Cheap Thrills Toronto

OTHER TITLES IN THE SERIES

Cheap Thrills

TORONTO

Great Toronto meals
for under $15.00

[2002-2003]

Nancy Marrelli
& Simon Dardick

Véhicule Press

Special thanks to Vicki Marcok, Matt Huculak,
Bruce Henry, Theresa Rowat, Paul Parenteau, Albert Tan,
and Margot Glatt.

Véhicule Press acknowledges the support of the
Government of Canada's Book Industry
Development Program

Cover illustration: Laurie Lafrance
Cover art direction and design: JW Stewart
Inside imaging: Simon Garamond
Printing: AGMV-Marquis Inc.

CATALOGUING IN PUBLICATION DATA

Nancy Marrelli & Simon Dardick
Cheap thrills Toronto : great Toronto meals
for under $15

ISBN 1-55065-154-4

1. Restaurants–Ontario–Toronto–Guidebooks.
I. Marrelli, Nancy. II. Dardick, Simon, 1943-

TX907.5 C22 T67 2001   647.95713'541

Published by Véhicule Press
P.O.B. 125, Place du Parc Station
Montréal, Québec H2X 4A3

514-844-6073   FAX 514-844-7543

www.vehiculepress.com
www.cheapthrillsguides.com

U.S. DISTRIBUTION
Independent Publishers Group, Chicago, Illinois.

Printed in Canada

Contents

What is a Cheap Thrill?

The restaurants in this book generally offer meals at dinner for $15 or less. This does not mean that every meal in the restaurant will be under $15, but there should be a reasonable selection in that price range before taxes, tip, and alcohol.

Independent Reviews

We pride ourselves on the independence of our reviews. No offers of free food or any other gratuities are ever accepted by our reviewers.

Check it Out Before You Go

Restaurants change constantly—menus, hours, and owners are in constant flux. The information in this book was current at the time of publication, but there's no guarantee that things won't change without warning. It's a good idea to call ahead.

**This book would not be possible without
our reviewers and contributors...**

Nancye Appleby
David Balzer
Gerry Barr
Gwynne Basen
Yvonne Bialowas
Medbh Bidwell
Sarah Brierley
Abigail Brodovitch
Heather Bruder
Suzanne E. Campbell
Demetra Christakos
Barbara Craig
Paul Craig
Simon Dardick
Beverley Daurio
Susan Donais
Jonah Engle
Ivan English
Marijke Friesen
Margot Glatt
Susan Glickman
Kevin Goble
Harvey Hamburg
Bruce Henry
Irena Jares
Jennifer Jennings
Pamela Kanter
Robert Kasher
Laurie Lafrance
Laura Lush
Rod MacRae
Sandra Marcok
Philippe Marcoux

Heather Marrelli
John Marrelli
Nancy Marrelli
Roger Marrelli
Pedro Mendes
Catherine Mitchell
Paul V. Parenteau
Rosalba Perrotta
Milka Popov
Pearl Quong
Dahlia Riback
Ed Rothberg
Theresa Rowat
Richard Sanger
Dorothea Schramm
Ellen Servinis
Martha Sharpe
Greg Shaw
Kate Sigurdson
Monique Smith
Christine Sternberg
Ricardo Sternberg
Albert Tan
Rhea Tregebov
Carole Welp
Alana Wilcox
Rex Williams
Margie Wolfe

Introduction

Toronto is a city with many different food stories. You can eat well on many different scales, and in virtually every corner of the metro area. There are fine and fancy eateries with upscale atmosphere and refined ingredients, but also a broad selection of places where you can eat extremely well for much less. This book is about affordable places that serve wonderful and varied food from all corners of the globe. The striking multi-cultural mix of the food available in this ever-changing city reflects the origins of people who have chosen to live here but who have links to other lands, cultures, and cuisines. These exist quite comfortably with many excellent but humble classic home-style foods. *Cheap Thrills* restaurants are not places with endless similar versions of overpriced, trendy food served in small quantities on large white plates, where more attention is paid to décor than to the food. You will find cuisines and dishes that will be familiar and things that may be new to you. *Cheap Thrills* restaurants are downtown, uptown, in the suburbs, in chi-chi neighbourhoods, and in strip malls—an emerging place for good food because of their proximity to where people live and eat.

We all need cheap thrills. We're busy. We work hard, juggling the various parts of our lives. We work late. We have responsibilities. We don't have time to shop. We cook on weekends, if at all. There's not enough time to do it all.

Our eating habits have changed. Often, we just can't face the prospect of putting together a meal. We eat out or we do take-out at the end of a difficult day. We travel and need to quickly and efficiently find good affordable places to eat in unfamiliar territory. More and more we also love to eat out for the adventure and the pleasure of it. We frequently want to eat out without totally blowing the budget, but we want good, interesting food and a decent environment. We want a Cheap Thrill!

Many of us are in a rut, not necessarily a bad rut, just boring.

We have our familiar inexpensive restaurants where we go again and again because the food is good, the service is friendly, and the prices are affordable. But new alternatives would certainly be welcome. It seems to be a good idea to share each other's good and inexpensive standbys. A guide to people's favourite places was born from this idea. *Cheap Thrills* guides to Montreal and New York City have been resounding successes. It was time to do Toronto.

We asked Torontonians from all parts of the city, and in many walks of life, to share their favourite low-cost restaurant with us. The ground rules were simple. The food had to be good, and the prices had to be about $15 or less for dinner, before taxes, tip, and alcohol. The response has been great! People are eager to share information about their favourite inexpensive haunts.

The list of reviewers and contributors is in the front of the book. We thank all our reviewers for their good appetite, judgement, and willingness to share favourite spots. Margo Glatt and Albert Tan have been especially helpful, and Theresa Rowat and Paul Parenteau have made significant contributions to this book in so many different ways. Their support and collaboration are much appreciated.

This edition includes 90 *Cheap Thrills*, some with multiple locations. These are restaurants where you can get a good meal at a good price, with kids or without, alone or with friends.

Cheap Thrills is a celebration of the amazing diversity of Toronto. The restaurant owners and chefs in this book are anxious to share their traditions and cuisine with us. *Cheap Thrills Toronto* is a reminder that good food is about the *joy of eating*, the pleasure we all get when we bite into something that tastes delicious and is satisfying. Whether you grew up inToronto, are a recent arrival or visiting, get out there and explore the culinary bounty of Toronto.

Alphabetical Listing of Restaurants

Amato

429 Yonge St. (at College)
Subway: Carlton
Phone: 416.977.8989
Hours: Mon-Sun 11am-2am; deliveries until 4am
Credit cards: V, MC; Alcohol: beer only
Wheelchair access: no
Average slice of pizza: $3.50
Plus 5 other locations: **534 Queen St. W., 380 College St.,**
   238 Queen W., 700 Lawrence W., 672 St. Clair Ave. W.

Amato serves great pizza-by-the-slice in six locations around Toronto.

The main attraction is Real Deal Pizza, by the slice or made to order. Pizza is their business and they are experts: great crust, fresh baked texture, a perfectl oil-glazed (but not greasy) bottom, and a slightly puffed light body. Slices are heavy on the veg or meat toppings rather than the cheese and tomato, perfect to eat out of hand without utensils. If you want more cheese order a double cheese topping. Pizza-by-the-slice is pre-made, with about 20 combos displayed in showcases. There are basic or gourmet options, many vegetarian. Slices are generous, and they pop your choice into a very hot oven to crisp it. Primavera with olive oil and veggies is a good bet. Made-to-order pizzas come with classic toppings or more adventurous choices. The Calabrese with tomato sauce, spicy sopressato, mozzarella, and roasted peppers is delightful. Gorgonzola adds spin to this favourite.

Gino Amato, a baker from Molise, and his three sons opened a small spot on Yonge in 1995. It was good, and customers clamoured for other Toronto locations, so they multiplied this winning neighbourhood pizza business. Gino is gone, but sons Massimo, Giuseppe, and Walter run the whole show (no franchises), keeping arrangements simple but the food good. These are not dining rooms but places where you go to munch and move on, or do take-out. They stay open late and deliver even later. Amato's are well organized, efficient, and fast-food-rustic Italian. You're sure to find a pizza combo you'll love!

Annapurna Vegetarian Restaurant

1085 Bathurst St. (at Dupont)
Subway: Dupont or Bathurst streetcar north
Phone: 416.537.8513
Hours: Mon-Sat 11:30am-9pm; Wed 11:30am-6:30pm; closed
 Sunday
Credit cards: V, MC, Interac; Alcohol: no
Wheelchair access: entrance yes; restroom no
Average main course: $6

Annapurna is a peaceful vegetarian haven on the fringes of
the Annex.

The menu is vegetarian with dairy products clearly
indicated so you can choose vegan dishes if you prefer. There
are South Indian specialties, Asian-influenced dishes, and
North American health food items. House-made soups are
always hearty and satisfying. One of the samplers is a good
way to try little bits of different dishes like potato *masala*,
vegetable curry with spinach and coconut (*sagu*), *sambar*
(lentils) and organic brown rice, served with yogurt, chapatti,
pappadum, pickles, and chutneys. It's a varied mix of lightly
spiced flavours and textures that mix and match well with
the fixings. The *bhajia* appetizer is a generous portion of deep
fried (but not greasy) vegetables in batter served with the
kitchen's own outstanding tamarind chutney, a skilled blend
of sweet and sour. South Indian dosas, crepes made from rice
and lentil flour, are also available. Other choices include
dressed baked potatoes, tofu burgers and hotdogs, and an
organic brown rice macro plate. Yogurt drinks, cold or hot
apple cider, and special herbal teas are good for you and they
are tasty as well.

Annapurna was founded in 1974 by the followers of New-
York-based Indian spiritual leader Sri Chinmoy. "Annapurna"
means Goddess of the Harvests, and is also the name of an
8,000+ metre-high mountain in North-central Nepal. It is
bright, serene, non-smoking, and is run by Shivaram Trichur
and Deva Vira. They offer free meditation courses and there
are videos of Sri Chinmoy. Annapurna serves delicious and
nutritious food that leaves you feeling good too.

Artful Dodger

10 Isabella St. (at Yonge)
Subway: Bloor
Phone: 416.964.9511
Hours: Mon-Sun 11am-2am
Credit cards: V, MC, Amex; Alcohol: all
Wheelchair access: no
Average main course: $8

The Artful Dodger serves up typical friendly pub ambiance and freshly-made pub food in the Yonge/Bloor area, and the price is right too!

The daily specials include soup and sandwiches, pasta, pizza, or full meals like roast lamb, and they are particularly good choices. The set special on Saturday evening is NY Peppercorn steak and on Sunday evening there's wonderful prime rib with classic Yorkshire pudding. The weekend Bulldog Breakfast (11am-4pm) for the Big Hungry has three eggs, bacon, sausage, beans, and homefries. They have a wide selection of local and imported beers on tap. The garlic bread, bruschetta, and wings are great appetizers that could also be satisfying snacks with a beer. The British-style fish and chips are tasty with homecut fries, and the burgers are fresh and juicy. This is pub food at its best, in the time-honored tradition.

No one quite remembers when the Artful Dodger opened—some time around 1974 when a hair salon was transformed into the pub in this 3-storey semi-detached double. Current owners, Michael Henry and Tom Nasterevi, maintain a comfortable and friendly place where the service is efficient and the food is freshly-prepared and really good. The décor is in keeping with the mid-19th century of Dickens' Artful Dodger. The main floor is non-smoking, kids are allowed on the outdoor patio only, and the clientele is an interesting mix of young and old, men and women. Peak times can be busy and somewhat noisy. The prices are amazing and the quality of the food is excellent.

Aunties and Uncles

74 Lippincott (near Bathurst)
Subway: Bathurst, then Bathurst streetcar south to College
Phone: 416.324.1375
Hours: Tue-Sun 9am-6pm
Credit cards: cash only; Alcohol: no
Wheelchair access: no
200 Bathurst (at Queen)
Subway: Bathurst, then Bathurst streetcar south to Queen
Phone: 416.703.9378
Hours: Dinner only; Tue-Thur & Sun 5pm-10pm;
   until 11pm Fri & Sat
Credit cards: V, MC, Diners, Interac; Alcohol: all
Average main course: breakfast $6.25, dinner $10

Aunties and Uncles delivers a great bang for the buck with
deeply satisfying food at two hip and shabby-chic spaces.

Lippincott serves brunch food that makes the grade any
time of day. Fluffy Belgian waffles with maple syrup and fresh
fruit are made from scratch—get there early on weekends
before they run out! The focaccia breakfast pocket combines
perfectly-scrambled eggs, lean bacon, caramelized onions, and
yummy aioli. Grilled cheddar and tomato sandwich on
challah is doubly delicious with peameal bacon. *Pan bagnat*
will transport you to the South of France! Bathurst offers diner
food at its comforting best. Mac and cheese is rich and creamy
cheddar, Swiss, peccorino, and blue cheeses with bacon if you
wish. Angel hair pasta with veggies, herbs, and garlic, steak/
frites, and pork chops—they're all winners! Aunties and
Uncles emphasize simple food with quality ingredients, and
fine touches like homemade ketchup and preserves. Coffee is
diner-style-good with free refills.

David Ginsberg and Russell Nicholls (head chef) opened
on Lippincott in 1998, and on Bathurst in 2001. Décor in
both locations is perfect retro fifties with arborite, chrome,
vinyl booths, and mismatched vinyl and bentwood chairs, all
with the very best Value Village patina. It's busy and noisy on
weekends but staff is helpful, attentive and Funny! Both
locations are comfy and hip retro diners with unpretentious
good food and some welcome finishing touches.

The Bishop & the Belcher

361 Queen St. W. (bet. John St. & Peter St.)
Subway: Osgoode
Phone: 416.591.2352
Hours: Sun-Thur 11:30am-1am; until 2am Fri & Sat
Credit cards: V, MC, Amex, Interac; Alcohol: all
Wheelchair access: no
Average main course: $7.95

The Bishop & the Belcher is a Queen Street West British-style pub without attitude!

Fries are fantastic—fresh cut with skins and cooked to perfection in vegetable oil. Typical pub fare is very nicely done here and they even have some "Bombay specials." Buffalo wings are the jumbo variety, (mild to hot or honey garlic) with a real blue cheese dressing. They're tangy, crisp outside and moist and tender inside—available daily but they're also the Sunday special. Fish and chips deliver a generous melt-in-your-mouth portion of flaky halibut in light and crispy beer batter. The calamari is tender (not rubbery), deep-fried in a light tempura-style batter and served with a delicate curry/mayo dip. The Bishop burger is a large and juicy home-style char-grilled patty lightly spiced with garlic and black pepper. You can add extra toppings and/or dress with one of the fancy mustards available. The daily specials are a good deal. Weekend brunch is standard English fry-up.

Sisters Anita and Jennifer Gill started the pub in 1994. Anita is a professional chef and she trains and supervises the kitchen staff. Their hands-on approach really makes a difference. Service is efficient and welcoming, with many regulars. There's a patio out back. The décor is decorative anglophilia with a large stone fireplace at the back. They have Trivial Pursuit cards at each table and games such as Boggle, Scrabble, checkers and Battleship to entertain. It can get smoky as the evening progresses. An extensive selection of beers is available on tap. Incidentally they have a superb Thanksgiving dinner. This is a thoroughly pleasant pub with really satisfying food and no pretence.

Bitondo Pizzeria & Sandwiches

11 Clinton St. (south of College)
Streetcar: College
Phone: 416.533.4101
Hours: Sun-Thur 11am to midnight; until 12:30am Fri;
    until 1am Sat
Credit cards: cash only; Alcohol: no
Wheelchair access: no
Prices: Pizza $8.45-$12.95, sandwiches $2.60-$4.95, pasta $5-$6

Bitondo has scrumptious Italian take-out and you can eat in too at this old-time Little Italy location that is a late-night favourite.

The all-Italian menu fits on the back of their business card—and it includes only the best of the easy and portable. They do a few things very well indeed! The house specialties are panzerotti, pizza and the wonderful veal sandwiches with hot or sweet peppers and sauce. Veal scallopini is enormous, served on a fresh Kaiser bun imbued with the delicious sauce. The pizza has an extraordinarily good chewy thin crust and is available with a choice of cheese, pepperoni, green pepper, and mushroom topping. This is not the place for designer pizza, but it's always done right, just as your Italian grand-mother would do it. Forget the fancy stuff, they go for the good! They also serve sausage sandwiches, meatballs, and various pastas including a sensational lasagne. Everything here is made from scratch. If you want coffee and dessert, drop by "The Dip" up the street at 594 College (*See p. 26*).

The Bitondo family began the business in 1966 and they still run it, changing almost nothing since the beginning. This is not the place for a blow-out date or special occasion. They do mostly take-out and catering and the interior is almost "anti-décor," but if you want to eat-in they do have four tables, orange plastic chairs and a "Countertop Champion" video-game. Bitondo's has a modest selection of real Italian food at very affordable prices. You will find yourself coming back again and again because they do the basics so very well.

Biryani House

6 Roy's Square (at Yonge & Bloor)
Subway: Bloor
Phone: 416.927.9340
Hours: Mon-Thur 11:30am-9:30pm; until 10pm Fri & Sat
Credit cards: V, MC, Amex, Interac; Alcohol: all
Wheelchair access: no
Average main course: $7.50

Biryani House near Yonge and Bloor is a jewel of a place serving excellent North Indian food at very modest prices.

Biryani is the house specialty, of course, but they also have kebabs, tandoori dishes and curries. The biryanis are a winning combo of fluffy basmati rice and mixed vegetables with chicken, lamb, or beef pulled together with a masterful combination of spices. The whole dish is finished with great toppings like fresh roasted nuts, mint sauce, and fried onions. The court-style moghul dishes are richly garnished with spices and nuts. The butter chicken is a particularly good choice, redolent with ginger, cinnamon, and green chilli. The pakora basket is a superb opener with a tart tamarind sauce. In addition to North Indian specialties Biryani House offers *sultaani chaap*, a Hyderabad specialty of excellent grilled marinated lamb, vinegary/hot beef *vindaloo*, some Indian-inspired salmon dishes, and other goodies. Ingredients are fresh, dishes are attractively presented, and fragrant spices are applied with just the right touch by a knowing hand. Lunch specials are an incredible deal!

Chef Debu Saha is master of the open kitchen. Modest but pleasant décor make for a homey ambiance, aspiring to upscale. There are a few sidewalk tables in good weather. It can get crowded at lunch but it's pleasant. Biryani House is a perfect choice for a quick lunch or for a more relaxed meal after work. It makes an affordable indulgence combined with a movie, a visit to the Toronto Reference Library, browsing at Holt Renfrew, or hunting for affordable chic at nearby Holt Renfrew Home.

Blue Bay Café

2243 Dundas St. W.
Streetcar: Dundas Main Station
Phone: 416.533.8838
Hours: Tue-Sun 5-10pm
Credit cards: V, MC, Amex, Diners; Alcohol: all
Wheelchair access: yes
Average main course: $11

Blue Bay Café on Dundas West serves the delicious and unusual food of Mauritius.

The Daube of chicken is a spectacular stew with a rich, flavourful, and beautifully-spiced sauce. Fish and seafood are special features of this cuisine and the presentation is invariably simple, light, and utterly fresh. Fish *vindaye* with mustard, and the fish with ginger sauce are both special treats, adding transparent layers of flavour to the goodness of fresh fish cooked just so. Curried shrimp with green mango or shrimp *mascarenas* with rich tomato sauce are good choices. Main courses come with rice, salted coleslaw, fresh tomato salsa and a particularly yummy hot sauce. Dishes are prepared with simple elegance, leaving the natural flavours and textures of the food to shine through. The Island of Mauritius is in the Indian Ocean, near Madagascar and its influences are East Indian, French, African, Creole, and Chinese. The cuisine is a wonderful hybrid with exotic touches of all these.

Blue Bay has been part of the Toronto food scene since 1985 and it's been a long-time West End favourite for very good reason. It's a good choice as a date place, with cloth tablecloths and napkins. Decoration is simple with a nautical theme, and everything is spotlessly clean. Service is friendly and efficient. It's worth going out of your way for the special tastes at Blue Bay.

Butler's Pantry

371 Roncesvalles Ave. (at Grenadier Rd.)
Subway: Dundas West
Phone: 416.537.7750
Hours: Mon-Thur 10am-11pm; until 12:30am Fri & Sat; until
   10:30pm Sun
Credit cards: V, MC, Amex; Alcohol: no
Wheelchair access: entrance yes; restroom no
Average main course: $6.95

Butler's Pantry, an eclectic multi-ethnic bistro with un-pretentious home-style cooking, is a Roncesvalles institution.

The menu includes house versions of dishes from Korea, France, India, Morocco, Burma, Greece, and who knows where else! Most dishes are served with a fresh salad and a little jug of fabulous house dressing. *Khowsway* is a yummy Burmese chicken dish with coconut milk served on egg noodles with coriander. The Moroccan chicken *bastilla* is a flaky filo pastry with a cinnamon-scented filling of chicken, mushrooms, egg, and almonds. The lamb moussaka is a piping hot plate of beautifully sauced and seasoned layers of eggplant, lamb, and feta with browned creamy potatoes. Other favourites include shepherd's pie, beef Burgundy, and a broccoli-cheddar quiche. Homemade desserts are decadent, delicious, and very affordable. Brunch is available daily and includes French toast (with fresh fruit, whipped cream and maple syrup) and eggs Benedict with optional smoked salmon.

Butler's Pantry has been around since the early 1980s, and current owners Atique and Maha Azad maintain the long-established friendly and unassuming atmosphere, broad-based menu, and very reasonable prices. Changing local art decorates the funky orange walls and a large collection of teapots adorns cupboard shelving in the front room. Staff are very accommodating, the atmosphere is unrushed but everything moves along like a well-rehearsed symphony. Head to Roncesvalles and Butler's Pantry for a gastronomic trip around the world on a shoestring budget.

Café Diplomatico

594 College St. (at Clinton)
Subway: College, then take College streetcar westbound
Phone: 416.534.4637
Hours: Mon-Sun 8am-1:30am
Credit cards: V, MC, Amex; Alcohol: all
Wheelchair access: entrance yes; restroom no
Average main course: $7.95

Café Diplomatico, affectionately known as "The Dip," in the heart of Little Italy is a classic Italian family restaurant with great prices.

Fixed daily specials Monday through Friday are a terrific choice, offering pasta in several guises, with fried calamari and shrimp or pasta with seafood and white wine on Fridays. Or you can match a favourite pasta (including linguine, tortellini, ravioli, rigatoni) to your choice of sauce including spicy vegetarian, rosé, vodka, meat, etc. Pastas are fresh and cooked just right, and the sauces are all you would expect from a savvy kitchen that uses quality ingredients respectfully. The Alfredo and *vongole* (clams) with white wine sauces are recommended. Excellent chicken parmesan is served with a generous green salad and fries from heaven—thick-cut ridged potatoes so fresh they are almost sweet, crisp outside and tender inside. These fries are worth the calories! They also serve homemade soups: pasta e fagioli, minestrone, and simple, elegant stracciatella. Breakfast is available ($1 more after noon) as are panini, pizza, panzerotto and calzone. Cannoli or biscotti are a fine finish or splurge on sfogliatella. The coffee is smooth and delicious, their own mix of Caruso and Cimo.

The Dip has been around since 1968 and the Mastrangelo family knows what it's doing. Good weather brings what may be the best patio in Toronto, with great people watching onto College. Service is excellent and kids are welcome, although this is also a great place for a special night out on a budget. There's a light and airy feeling to The Dip with its marble-topped tables and huge windows—and food from an Italian nonna's kitchen!

Caramba Restaurant & Latin Grill

394 Pacific Ave. (at Dundas St. W.)
Subway: Dundas West
Phone: 416.604.4844
Hours: Tue-Fri 12pm-11pm; Sat 10am-11pm;
  Sun 10am-10pm; closed Monday
Credit cards: V. MC, Amex, Diners, Interac; Alcohol: all
Wheelchair access: entrance yes; restroom no
Average main course: $12.99

Caramba is a comfortable family-style Peruvian grill on the West Side near Dundas.

Fried or grilled fish and seafood and grilled meats are the house specialties. The food is done simply Peruvian style and it is GOOD! Portions are very generous and can definitely be shared except for the biggest appetites. A good plan is to go in a group and share a variety of appetizers and main courses. The *jalea* platter is a heap of lightly-battered and tender calamari, shrimp, and thin fillets of whitefish, with potato, sliced onion, and cilantro. Typical latino sides include rice, yucca and plantains, and, of course, potatoes which are native to Peru. The house salsa is fresh, hot, and delicious—a smooth blend of Scotch bonnets and olive oil with lots of taste and plenty of heat. The *tacu tacu* is crusted fried white beans with rice that you can order with salad, eggs, or steak. Good choices are any of the fried or grilled fish dishes that work so well with the wonderful salsa. Grilled chicken or marinated steak is featured in several dishes. The *empanada de platano* is a Peruvian dessert specialty, made with plantain and creamy rice pudding. Weekend brunch specials include very good *huevos rancheros*.

Caramba is a low-key and casual place. Décor is not their strong suit but the food is well prepared, fresh and not unnecessarily complicated. Chef-owner Olga Teruya opened Caramba in 1999 and it's become a neighbourhood favourite for reliably good Peruvian food and great prices. Kids and families are welcome, as are solo diners.

Centre Street Deli

1136 Centre St. (bet. Bathurst & Dufferin St.), Thornhill
Subway: no subway; call for directions
Phone: 905.731.8037
Hours: Mon-Sun 7am-8pm
Credit cards: V, MC, Diners, Interac; Alcohol: beer & wine
Wheelchair access: yes
Smoked meat sandwich: $5.95-$6.95

Centre Street Deli in Thornhill is the place to go for Montreal-style smoked meat and other deli treats.

Deli delights include matzo ball soup, great chopped liver, karnatzel, and home-style Jewish specialties like gefilte fish, cabbage rolls, smoked fish, latkes, blintzes, and knishes. It's all good stick-to-your ribs food. Enjoy yourself—then go back to watching your diet tomorrow. The specialty of the house without question is Lester's from Montreal smoked meat on rye, or a platter but that's *really* an indulgence! It's tender, moist, nicely spiced, and deeply satisfying! It comes mild or old fashioned—spice encrusted old fashioned is most popular. Fries are fresh, not frozen, and cooked in vegetable oil. There's a children's menu (12 and under). If you can manage it there are desserts like rice pudding, strudel, cheesecake and apple pie with ice cream. They do lots of take-out and the catered party sandwiches will ratchet up your popularity by several points. They're not gussied up—kind of like what your mom might have made for a birthday party.

Centre Street Deli was opened in 1988 by Cheryl Morantz with Sam and Tom Agelopoulos (her family is from Snowdon Deli in Montreal). They expanded to this location in 1999. Customers know exactly how this food should taste and they'd be out of business if it didn't cut the mustard. They've got it right and they have a happy and loyal clientele, from kids to grandmothers. Décor is not fancy and it can get busy at peak times but it's big, clean, and friendly—like a deli should be.

Chopan Kebab House

798 Danforth Ave. (at Woodycrest Ave.)
Subway: Pape
Phone: 416.778.1200
Hours: Mon-Fri 11am-12am; until 2am Sat & Sun
Credit cards: V, MC, Amex, Interac; Alcohol: no
Wheelchair access: no
Average main course: $9.99

The Chopan Kebab House on Danforth near Pape has unique and delicious Afghan specialties.

The *mantu* appetizer is a must: a steamed dumpling topped with a rich and spicy mixture of ground beef and onions. You won't go wrong with one of their beautifully charbroiled kebabs of lamb, chicken or beef. The combos are a good way to have some variety, especially the *shami* combo that is wonderfully moist and flavourful. The dinners are also a good bet. *Qabeli pallow* is a heaping portion of basmati rice topped with raisins, carrots and almonds, hiding a surprise of juicy braised lamb. Some meals come with sensational *khassa* flatbread, made in-house. Okra, green beans, and potatoes are tasty but pass on the spinach. *Dough*, is a thick "drink" of yogurt, water, cucumber, mint and lots of salt—it's definitely not for the faint of heart! *Ferinee* is a pudding (there's also a frozen version) delicately and deliciously flavoured with rosewater, cardamom and saffron.

Chopan (the word means shepherd) Kebab House was founded in 1997 by Afghan Olympic wrestler Qayum Mohammed and Fada Alakoozi. Mohammed is no longer there but Alakoozi and his brother Nasir continue to offer an authentic Afghan menu using only halal meat. There's no alcohol or smoking. It's comfortable and there are traditional rugs but there's a little too much neon for a luxe and cosy atmosphere. It can get a bit noisy if there's a party downstairs. Chopan Kebab House is a delicious window into traditional Afghan cuisine—a lot easier than a trip to Kabul.

Churrasco Villa

254 Eglinton Ave. E. (at Mount Pleasant)
Subway: Eglinton
Phone: 416.487.7070
Hours: Mon-Thur 11am-10pm; until 11pm Fri; Sat 4pm-11pm;
Sun 4pm-10pm
Credit cards: V, MC, Amex, Interac; Alcohol: all
Wheelchair access: yes
Quarter chicken meal: $9.95

Churrasco Villa in North Toronto is a Portuguese grill haven.

Food is grilled simply but expertly on natural wood charcoal, charred, cooked to the point of perfection, and basted with piri-piri spices. The most popular dish is the quarter chicken, a generous serving with two sides chosen from fresh cut fries, roast potatoes, rice or steamed crunchy vegetables. Ribs, shrimp, and steak are over the *Cheap Thrills* limit but the chicken options are not—and portions are large so you can share a meal for two for a $5 plate charge. Or blow the budget on grilled salmon. Sandwiches are on crusty Portuguese buns, dressed with onions, peppers, mushrooms, with a salad on the side. Appetizers can be combined to make a meal with the daily soup. Grilled calamari or chicken wings with various levels of hot sauce are both great choices. This is not the ideal place for vegetarians but they do a delicious fire-grilled veggie platter tossed with balsamic vinaigrette. Grilled sardine aficionados will be very content. Take-out and doggie bags are very popular. Crème caramel tart is a good and modest dessert.

George Duarte and Tony Cappelano opened Churrasco Villa in 1999. George's father Alex Duarte owned the celebrated Churrasco at Dundas and Ossington until 1996. George and Tony were at the Wildfire Grill before opening here. They've assembled a winning operation—a friendly, comfortable, bustling place with an open grill and great atmosphere. Staff are attentive and helpful but not intrusive. It gets crowded at peak times. They're very kid-friendly. Churrasco Villa is about big quantities of great grill food at very reasonable prices.

Coconut Grove Roti Shop

183 Dundas St. W. (bet. University & Bay)
Subway: St. Patrick, or Dundas streetcar
Phone: 416.348.8887
Hours: Mon-Fri 10am-8pm; closed Saturday & Sunday
Credit cards: cash only; Alcohol: no
Wheelchair access: no
Average main course: $5.50

Coconut Grove is a dynamite Roti Shop Downtown, right near the Toronto bus terminal.

Rotis are the house speciality and they do them with great care and attention, Guyanese style. Any of the rotis is a meal in itself, a plump handful of delicious dough with a savoury filling. Fillings are tasty blends of veggies, chicken, beef or goat, beautifully sauced and spiced. The combo is a special treat (vegetarian) with potatoes, spinach, chickpeas, cabbage and eggplant. Add the house hot sauce, a sublime combo of powerful heat with that appealing chili taste. If you can resist the rotis you can try the excellent main dishes served with rice and beans: kingfish, jerk chicken, boneless curry chicken, oxtail, curry beef or goat. They use halal meat. The kitchen has a fine hand with vegetarian dishes. Plantain chips are always a treat.

Rafena Twahir and her husband Mohamed Rahman own and operate this gem of a spot that Rafena's parents originally started. Bibi has taken over the kitchen from Rafena's mom and she sees to it that nothing but good food comes out of this kitchen. The many hospital employees in this area are regulars. Coconut Grove is mainly a take-out place, but there is seating, albeit not luxurious. (Note that they are closed weekends.) They set a high standard for roti!

Country Style Hungarian

450 Bloor St. W. (at Bathurst)
Subway: Bathurst
Phone: 416.537.1745
Hours: Mon-Sun 11am-10pm
Credit cards: cash only; Alcohol: no
Wheelchair access: entrance yes; restroom no
Average main course: $10.50 including taxes

Country Style Hungarian on Bloor near Bathurst serves no-frills Hungarian comfort food.

The menu includes all the rib-sticking specialties you would expect to find in Budapest. Fixed specials change daily and include a hearty soup, a meat stew, and cabbage rolls every day. And what cabbage rolls they are—neatly rolled plump juicy bundles of meat, rice and flavour!!! Soups include chicken (sometimes with liver dumplings), beef noodle, goulash, mushroom, etc.—a meal in itself with excellent rye bread. Main courses include chicken paprikash with a rich sour cream sauce, and a fine wiener schnitzel. Vegetables are not the strong suit but you won't go wrong with pickled beets, coleslaw, potatoes and dumplings. On Saturday and Sunday expect roast duck, stuffed chicken, and beef with paprikash onions. There are a few vegetarian choices such as noodles with cottage cheese or ground walnuts and wonderful dessert crepes filled with jam, cheese, or nuts. Everything has the good solid taste of home cooking and portions are very generous. Bubbly raspberry soda goes down well with it all and homemade strudels are perfect if you have room.

Country Style Hungarian has fed many generations of hungry patrons on a budget. It grew out of a delicatessen that opened in the 1950s and slowly evolved into a restaurant. Current owners Judy and Frank Pek are very hands on and keep everything running smoothly—Judy has been here for 23 years! The décor won't win design awards but the food is satisfying and plentiful. Staff are efficient but it can be noisy at peak times. This is one of the best buys in town—you definitely won't leave hungry!

Dai Nam

221 Spadina Ave. (at Sullivan St.)
Streetcar: Either Queen or Dundas West
Phone: 416.598.3805
Hours: Sun-Thur 10am-10pm; until 12am Fri & Sat
Credit cards: MC, Amex, Interac; Alcohol: all
Wheelchair access: yes; restroom no
Average main course: $8

Dai Nam is a Vietnamese restaurant in Chinatown with a wide offering of superb food.

The menu is huge and varied and all of it is good! Rice paper wraps are a house specialty. The wraps arrive in a stack of plates—one wrap per plate—with fillings of your choice and crudités on the side, and you build your own meal or snack of tasty little packets. A small order is 5 wraps; a medium is 10. The grilled oyster appetizer with buttered breadcrumbs is so plump and juicy it will make you swoon! Crab in season is a great choice, especially spicy black pepper crab. Hot and sour soup with seafood, fish, shrimp, or chicken is a meal in a bowl. Veggies are treated respectfully and arrive crisp and fresh. The grilled pork chop with lemongrass is tender, juicy, and packed with flavour. Coconut, mango, or avocado milk shakes are big favourites. Rack of lamb is outside the *Cheap Thrills* boundaries but is beautifully prepared. Vegetarian choices are available.

This family-owned restaurant opened in 1997, and is named after a four-year old son. Saigon émigrés Anh and her brother are out front and husband Khanh is in the kitchen, taught by his father, a gifted home cook. They are unfailingly helpful and accommodating. The décor is typical Chinatown, and there's a pleasant feel to the place. This is a good spot for a family or a crowd who want to share. And those grilled oysters are seriously good, and addictive too!

Daily Sushi Japanese Restaurant

20 Carlton St. (at Yonge)
Subway: College
Phone: 416.977.4333
Hours: Mon-Fri 11am-11pm; Sat 11:30 am-11pm;
    Sun 4:30pm-11pm
Credit cards: V, MC, Amex, Interac; Alcohol: beer & wine
Wheelchair access: entrance yes; restroom no
Average main course: $12.00

Daily Sushi Japanese Restaurant is a modest little place near the old Maple Leaf Gardens where sushi is king!

Sushi and sashimi is what it's really all about here. The menu is extensive and daily board specials range from teriyaki to exotic eel. There is a great choice of combination plates that come with miso soup and salad. You won't leave hungry with the Bay Street combo and its selection of tuna, salmon, yellowtail, red snapper, shrimp, and crab sashimi, a handroll, plus cucumber and salmon rolls (3 each). Although a bit smaller, the Yonge Street combo of sashimi and a California roll will be sure to satisfy. Ambitious appetites can opt for the C.N. Tower! ($29.99 for two).

You can choose from Daily Sushi's extensive list of sushi and sashimi or order such favourites as salmon teriyaki and teppanyaki beef. The bento box selections are as attractive to the eye as they are to the palate. The vegetarian sushi set is popular, as are the hot pot noodles: udon noodles in a delicious chicken or beef broth replete with tempura shrimp, chicken, egg, mushrooms, and vegetables.

There is are a wide selection of lunch specials ($4.99-$5.99) that are served until 3pm. They offer a 15% discount for takeout and do a brisk business at lunch time.

Daily Sushi is the place to go whether you want a simple bowl of udon noodles or one of their fabulous combo plates. It's also perfect for a pre-movie dinner before you go to the Carlton cinema, which is right next door.

Dangerous Dan's Diner

714 Queen St. E. (at Broadview)
Streetcars: 501, 502, 504, 505 (from Queen or Broadview station)
Phone: 416.463.7310
Hours: Sun-Thur 11am-midnight; until 1am Fri & Sat
Credit cards: Visa only; Alcohol: all
Wheelchair access: entrance yes; restroom no
Average main course: $7, hamburger $4-$5

Dangerous Dan's Diner (Queen/Broadview) is about big value meals, burgers, hot sandwiches, and excessive desserts.

The menu is straightforward diner fare, portions are hefty, with lots of condiments. The big sellers are the burgers. They're big and bad! This is a juicy home-style burger with texture and taste, and all the fixings you could possibly want. There are also steak sandwiches on a Kaiser bun, rib sandwiches with mushrooms and onions on a poppy seed egg bun, and double layer grilled cheese sandwiches with bacon on thick-cut white or brown bread. Fish and chips, and pork chops with gravy or applesauce are available as well. Large steak dinners are outside the *Cheap Thrills* guidelines, but there's a Double D Beef Ribs dinner—2 ½ pounds of ribs with fries for $12.95, and a 24-ounce Homeburger with fries and a pop for $10.95, or a Coronary Burger—great for the lumberjacks in your life! They use canola oil but, alas, the chunky fries are frozen. Roll right along to a dessert of Brownie Overload with ice cream, whipped cream and chocolate syrup or an Apple Crisp Catastrophe. Or you can opt for a home-made shake or float.

Dangerous Dan's opened in 1999, named for the owner's grandfather, whose photo is on the menu and the diner wall. The Double D is a genuine diner, a little rough around the edges, with a blackboard menu, a pile of newspapers for browsing, no patio, and a familiar and friendly atmosphere. Kids are welcome. They deliver noon to midnight. You're not allowed to leave here hungry, and it's oh so easy on the pocketbook!

Darvish

6087 Yonge St. (in the Yonge Plaza), North York
Subway: Finch
Phone: 416.226.9028
Hours: Mon-Sun noon-11pm
Credit cards: V, MC, Amex, Interac; Alcohol: all
Wheelchair access: entrance yes; restroom no
Average main course: $9.50

Darvish offers family-style Persian cooking in Newtonbrook, North York.

Fresh, warm Persian flat bread, crispy but with a soft interior, is included with all meals. A platter of fresh parsley, watercress, radish, and onion slices is served with many meals, a great, typical accompaniment. They sometimes have a daily special—be sure to ask. *Borani-E-spinach* is a heavenly cold dish with garlic, lemon and ubiquitous yogurt, perfect scooped up with the bread. The *chelo kebabs* (cooked rice/broiled meat) are very popular. Ground beef, rack of beef, or chicken are marinated before being skilfully grilled so they remain juicy and tasty. Some combo plates are available and provide a variety of tastes. Slow-simmered dishes such as the chicken *polo* are tender, beautifully-spiced, home-style dishes. Rice pairs well with the food and it can be saffron-flavoured, or served with amazingly good, tiny, tart, red barberries (*zereshk*). You may never be satisfied with plain rice again! Mahogany-coloured dried sumac is used liberally as a condiment, and is available on your table. It is citrusy and slightly woodsy—definitely worth a try! Bite-size baklava scented with rose is the perfect dessert.

Darvish was the first Iranian restaurant in Toronto when it opened in 1985. Owner-chef Aazam Alexania is a chef trained in her native Iran. It's a family affair, and Aazam's brother Ali runs the front; he is cordial, efficient, and pleased to provide information about the food. The TV at the back is reserved for hockey playoff games and World Cup Soccer. Darvish is a friendly family dining room serving delicious and distinctive Persian food.

Diana Sweets

939 Lawrence Ave. E. (at Don Mills Rd.)
Bus: 54 from Eglinton subway or 25 from Pape subway
Phone: 416.447.2931
Hours: Mon-Fri 8am-10pm; Sat 8am-9:30pm; Sun 8am-8:30pm
Credit cards: V, MC, Amex, En Route; Alcohol: all
Wheelchair access: yes
300 Borough Dr. (Scarborough Town Centre)
Phone: 416.296.5770
Credit cards: V, MC, Amex, En Route; Alcohol: all
Wheelchair access: yes
Average main course: $8.50

Diana Sweets offers quality meals for family-style dining at
Square One, Don Mills Shopping Centre, and Scarborough
Town Centre.

The specials of the day are up on the board. The hands
down winner here is the $12.95 roast beef dinner, three
courses and coffee/tea—wonderful value, and it arrives as
ordered, rare, medium, or well done, with traditional
Yorkshire pudding. The food is fresh and good but not fancy
or fussy—lettuce is iceberg rather than mesclun, and sauces
are not elaborate. Other specials might be salmon, veal, pasta,
or chicken popover, all done well but without fuss or fanfare.
They serve a generous breakfast, including excellent eggs
Benedict. The regular menu includes a wide selection of pasta,
souvlaki, fish and chips, salads and sandwiches. Best desserts
are warm bread pudding, and apple or bumbleberry pie.

The Boukydis family has been feeding Torontonians at
Diana Sweets since 1912, originally with a tearoom and
confectionary shop downtown on Yonge (closed since 1980).
There are now three locations in malls with easy access to
parking. They're busy so be sure to reserve, but the rush is
usually over by 8 p.m. Wait staff have been there forever, and
the whole operation runs like clockwork. The décor and
atmosphere are refined with big brass chandeliers and
tablecloths and cloth napkins at dinner. Many customers are
regulars but newcomers are very welcome. This is such good
value for quality comfort food that you'll find yourself coming
back again and again.

Dipamo's Barbeque

838 College St.
Subway: Ossington; then 63 bus south, or College streetcar
Phone: 416.532.8161
Hours: Mon-Thur 12pm-3pm & 5pm-9pm; Fri & Sat until 10pm
Credit cards: V, Interac; Alcohol: all
Wheelchair access: no
514 Eglinton West (at Heddington)
Subway: Eglinton
Phone: 416.483.4227
Hours: Mon-Sun 5pm-10:30pm
Credit cards: V, MC; Alcohol: all
Wheelchair access: no
Average main course: $11

Dipamo's is one of the few places in Canada for genuine Southern BBQ—now in Little Italy and Midtown!

Dipamo's does BBQ as it should be done—long slow cooking in a serious pit at low temperature, using fresh aromatic wood. (Ribs take 5-6 hours, brisket and pork shoulder 12-17 hours.) They make ribs, beef brisket, pulled pork, and BBQ chicken, sandwiches or plates, and all the traditional house-made sides: potato salad, baked beans, coleslaw, fries and hush puppies. The sauces (one sweet, one hot but not searing) are light on the tomato, with lots of flavour, but they let the rich smoke taste shine through.

Philip and Gloria Nyman opened Dipamo's in 1998. The Eglinton branch is new. He is pitmaster. Fabulous corn pancakes with cheese are her contribution—authentic Venezuelan *cachapas*. Native Torontonian Nyman ate his way through the Carolinas, Tennessee, Georgia, Texas, finally deciding on his own version of Kansas City style BBQ with a dry rub, applied after cooking. He started with a cast iron pit from Oklahoma Joe's but they have moved on to a larger rig. They use apple wood from Collingwood. Décor is basic — this place is about the food! If you've never had real BBQ you're in for a real treat. Get yourself over here and savour the meltingly tender meat cooked oh so slowly in its own juices with a pungent smoky edge. They do take-out and catering. *Real BBQ is not fast food*—and this is the Real Deal!

El Paisano Taqueria

1544 Queen St. W. (at Dowling)
Streetcar: 501 Queen; or Lansdowne bus
Phone: 416.534.1218
Hours: Tue-Fri 5-10pm; Sat & Sun 12-10pm
Credit cards: no; Alcohol: no
Wheelchair access: no
Average antojitos: $2

El Paisano Taqueria offers a delicious variety of tacos and other typically Mexican street foods in Parkdale.

The menu is an exceptional collection of small taste treats. You order as few or as many as your appetite dictates. The tacos are particularly good, light and not greasy, stuffed with chopped beef, pork, chicken or poblano pepper and wrapped in a soft corn tortilla. Deep fried *flautas* and *quesadillas* are also available. The ceviche is outstanding! It's hard to resist filling up on the wonderful chunky guacamole but be disciplined so you can try as many things as possible from this tantalizinging menu of *antojitos* (little cravings). You may want to have five or six different things as the portions are small. The dishes are all made mild and you add salsas to your preferred degree of hotness. Everything is made in-house, including the tortillas. Fresh tortillas add a whole other dimension to Mexican food. Be sure to leave room for the flan and fresh-ground cinnamon tea.

Rafael Perez-Morales wanted to open a fresh taco stand on the street but Toronto's bylaws would not allow it. Rafael and his wife decided to create their own street and they have transformed a small space into just that with painted housefronts, Mexican-style public square benches, and street names like Mexico Boulevard and Canada Avenue. Service is friendly and they are kid-friendly. You won't find better Mexican street food without hopping a plane and heading south!

El Sol

1448 Danforth Ave. (bet. Coxwell & Greenwood)
Subway: Coxwell
Phone: 416.405.8074
Hours: Tue-Sun 3pm-11pm; closed Monday
Credit cards: V, MC, Amex; Alcohol: all
Wheelchair access: yes
Average main course: $9

Take a trip to Northern Mexico at El Sol, just east of the Greek area of Danforth.

They serve distinctive Northern Mexican specialties with rice and refried beans. Fresh ingredients and careful preparation result in appealing layers of flavour and texture. The generous El Sol platter for two is a best bet: soft flour and crisp corn tortillas filled with shredded beef, chorizo, chicken, cheese, potatoes, and onions, and served with rice and refried beans. The *sopes* are a luscious house specialty— a tasty soft, thick corn tortilla filled with mushrooms, potatoes, and your choice of meat. The guacamole is unbelievably good—one of their signature dishes! Be adventurous and try the *nopalitos*, cactus with dressing on lettuce. Choose your poison from a splendid variety of homemade salsas ranging from mild to painfully hot. The sangria goes down oh so well, and the drinks are splendid tropical blends, perfect on a warm sunny day, or for *The Great Escape on a Budget* in the middle of the winter doldrums!

Yolanda Paez and her brothers and sisters run El Sol, using their mother's recipes and it's as authentic Mexican as you can get in Toronto. This family business is pleased and proud to share its cuisine and culture. Wonderful masks festooning the walls are well worth a look and some are for sale. It's a warm, pleasant space and they even provide a small selection of books on Mexican art and cuisine if you're inclined to browsing. Be sure to try the special drink invented by Yolanda—*Tacones Altos* (High Heels), a silky blend of Kahlua, vodka, rum, grenadine, and cream. It's dynamite! El Sol provides a quick glimpse into a complex cuisine and culture.

Ethiopian House

4 Irwin Ave. (at Yonge)
Subway: Wellesley
Phone: 416.923.5438
Hours: Mon-Sun 11am-1am
Credit cards: V, MC, Amex, Interac; Alcohol: all
Wheelchair access: no
Average main course: $8.95

Ethiopian House near Yonge and Wellesley serves traditional Ethiopian dishes in a casual and mellow converted downtown house.

The menu is traditional Ethiopian food, served Ethiopian style. The various dishes ordered are served on *injera*, a delicious and filling, slightly sour, spongy crêpe-like bread made with fermented tef, a millet-like grain. Instead of using cutlery, diners scoop up the food and the rich sauces with rolled up pieces of the *injera*. The dishes are beautifully scented with the *berberé* spices shared by Ethiopia's many ethnic groups. The ancient spice mixture adds an earthy complexity to the rich sauces that are a significant part of Ethiopian cooking. The vegetarian *bayaaynatu* platter is a super choice. It has seven different and delicious vegetable dishes (lentils, split peas, chickpeas, collard greens, beans, tomatoes, potatoes) with a cold lettuce/tomato salad in the centre of the *injera*. There are a variety of textures and tastes, and the spice ranges from warm to mild. Beef dishes are also good—be sure to indicate your preferred degree of heat. There's an impressive coffee ceremony if you want to be adventurous.

Servers wear traditional dress and they are welcoming, attentive and helpful about explaining how everything works. The atmosphere is homey and comfortable. The bottom floor of this converted house has a few tables and the upstairs has a larger section with a bar area appropriate for larger parties. There's also a patio in summer. Enjoy traditional Ethiopian food and hospitality just steps away from the heart of Toronto!

Feathers Brewpub & Single Malt Scotch Whiskey Bar

962 Kingston Rd. (at Scarborough Rd.)
Subway: Victoria Park
Phone: 416.694.0443
Hours: Sun-Tue 11am-12am; until 1am Wed-Sat
Credit cards: V, MC, Amex, Interac; Alcohol: all
Wheelchair access: yes
Average main course: $8, dinner special $12

Feathers is a pub in the Upper Beaches where typical English pub food is a great accompaniment to a remarkable collection of single malt scotch.

Everything is made from scratch except Dufflet's desserts. Excellent roast beef with all the trimmings is served Thursday through Saturday, in a 6- or 8-ounce portion, cooked exactly as you like it. The house specialties are pub staples like the divine beef stout pie. Steak and kidney pie is the genuine article, and cottage pie is lean ground beef with cheddar cheese, mashed potatoes, and vegetables. They serve real bangers and mash, and fish and chips. The burgers are juicy and fresh with many topping options and thick-cut fries are done in canola oil. You can go the lighter route too with excellent guacamole, attractively presented spinach salad, or veggie wraps. Feathers has a stunning collection of bargain-priced single malt scotch, many not available elsewhere, and they occasionally have a Whiskey Night ($35-$60).

Owner Ian Innes opened Feathers here in 1981. It's a warm, comfortable, and unpretentious place, not too crowded or noisy, welcoming and with many regulars. There's wood panelling, curtains, sofa seats, fresh flowers on every table, with polished and unobtrusive service so it's good for a special night out. The ventilation is excellent but there is smoking at the bar. Innes is always in search of fabulous malt scotch that he imports privately. This used to be a brew-pub but the affiliated microbrewery went out of business in 2001. Feathers offers good atmosphere, good food, good company, and all that single malt scotch if that's your passion.

Ferro

769 St. Clair Ave. W. (at Arlington)
Subway: St. Clair West
Phone: 416.654.9119
Hours: Mon-Tue 11am-1am; Fri until 2am; Sat 11:30am-2am;
    Sun 5pm-1am
Credit cards: V, MC, Amex; Alcohol: all
Wheelchair access: yes
Average pizza, panini: $9.50

Ferro is a neighbourhood institution offering pizza and panini on St. Clair West, and they serve more upscale dinners as well.

Pizza, panini and other goodies are the Real Scene here and they're worth a detour. Pizzas are thin-crust (or calzone) and cooked to perfection in a traditional wood-burning oven. Taste and texture are great, and toppings are fresh and nicely combined with special touches like the sharp bite of Asiago cheese, sweet grilled veggies or caramelized onions, the assertiveness of arugula, and hearty tuna, grilled chicken, capers, or smoked bacon. The salads are meals in themselves and include beautifully-dressed grilled chicken, veal or salmon. The antipasto is a huge wonder with cheese, meats and veggies. Panini compositions include a delightful medley of prosciutto, Brie, artichoke, arugula and olive paste—yummy. The risotto is creamy and simply divine! If you really want to blow the budget you can opt for the fancier dinner specials.

Carmen, Frank and Armando Pronesti opened Ferro in 1993 as a neighbourhood pizza place with pool tables (there's still one in the back). In the late 90s they upgraded the space, introducing the funky metal décor created by friends at Dynamic Iron. They added upscale dinners to the other items on the menu, which is now quite happily schizophrenic. The brothers are hands-on and they keep everything hopping. Ferro is a huge neighbourhood success: welcoming, noisy, hip, and amiable, with a lively bar scene, but also efficiently delivering quality food and wine at affordable prices.

Free Times Café

320 College St. (near Spadina)
Subway: Spadina, or College streetcar
Phone: 416.967.1078
Hours: Mon-Fri 11:30am-2am; Sat 11am-2am; Sun 11am-1am
   (Sunday brunch buffet 11am-3pm)
Credit cards: V, MC, Amex, Interac; Alcohol: all
Wheelchair access: no
Average main course: $9.50; Sunday brunch $15.95, or once
   through $12.95

Free Times Café on College near Spadina is a café/bistro with live music, poetry and stand-up comedy during the week and a traditional Jewish brunch/buffet on Sunday!

The weekday menu includes traditional chicken soup with matzo balls, Middle Eastern dishes like hummous, couscous, shishtaouk, falafel, and diner-type items like burgers, chicken wings, club sandwich and Caesar salad. Desserts include apple crisp, lemon poppyseed cake, and cheesecake. There are daily specials and dinner show packages. There's a Saturday night klezmer party with a special buffet and dancing (package deal $22.95). The Sunday buffet—aka Bella! Did Ya Eat?—is a cornucopia of traditional Jewish brunch foods such as smoked fish, blintzes, Middle Eastern specialties, latkes, couscous, herring, fruit, eggs, French toast on challah, fresh fruit and vegetables, and home-style desserts. Everything is comfort-food-good.

Free Times Café has been a Toronto mainstay for twenty years, with a long open-stage tradition on Monday night (sign-up at 7, startup at 8). Since 1997 owner Judy Perly has operated the enormously popular Sunday brunch buffet with homey Jewish cooking. This is a great place to go for fun and food any day of the week. The Sunday brunch is a wonderful treat with live Klezmer music on the side. It's a joyous and fun meal no matter what your age or background—with a very high Bubby-approval rating!

Golden Star

7123 Yonge St. (at Doncaster), Thornhill
Subway: Finch; then Yonge St. bus north
Phone: 905.889.6891
Hours: Mon-Thur 10am-midnight; until 1am Fri & Sat; Sun
11am-midnight
Credit cards: Interac only; Alcohol: beer & wine
Wheelchair access: no
All-Star burger: $4.25

Golden Star in Thornhill is a family-run burger mecca.

The menu is not extensive—this is a burger place and it
has no pretensions to being anything else. They do have a
very nice Steak-on-a-Kaiser, a quality 5-ounce ribeye from
Nortown Butcher. They also have grilled breast of chicken on
a bun with BBQ sauce, or you can get a pound of char-grilled
chicken wings (about 8 pieces). The double-decker grilled
cheese is a thick and cheesy classic on white bread. There are
Yves-brand veggie burgers if that's your style and regular
frozen meat type burgers but everyone ignores them. The
burger of choice is the homemade All Star burger—a juicy
and delicious 6-ounce char-grilled burger that's the pride of
the house. The BBQ sauce is the secret creation of original
owner Frank Doria. They dress the hamburger with your
choice of topping and, of course, the special sauce. Fries are
fresh cut daily and fried in vegetable oil. Forget dessert, have
a milk shake or drop into Chapters across the street and buy
a book instead.

Frank Doria started Golden Star in 1965 in this location.
There are red and grey booths, butcher-block tables, and a
long counter where you order food, cafeteria style. They have
outdoor seating in the warmer months. This is still a family
business run by son Frank Doria Jr. and family. They care
about what they do and it shows in everything about this
place. It's comfortable, relaxed, and the quality is consistent.
Many loyal fans go to great lengths to get their All-Star burger
fix. Bring on the burger sweepstakes—this one's a contender!

Gourmet Vegetarian Restaurant

280 West Beaver Creek Dr. (Unit #22-23), Richmond Hill
Subway: no subway; call for directions
Phone: 905.886.0680
Hours: Mon-Sun 11am-10:30pm
Credit cards: cash only; Alcohol: no
Wheelchair access: yes
Average main course: $8

Gourmet Vegetarian Restaurant in a Richmond Hill strip mall provides Chinese vegetarian food!

The immense Chinese/English menu has a multitude of combinations and permutations of basic good, fresh ingredients, *not* including meat or fish, although they do use fish and meat-flavoured gluten and bean curd very effectively in many dishes. Fortunately menu descriptions are clear rather than cryptic. Portions are generous and food is prepared fresh with good quality ingredients. Meal-in-a-bowl noodle dishes are a superb choice, as are any of the many rice + virtually-anything-your-heart-desires dishes. There are 55 deluxe veggie dishes! They have many rice congee choices, and they even do hot pots. Udon noodles with braised eggplant in BBQ sauce is a real winner. This food feels virtuous and healthy but they manage to do it all without compromising taste. Sauces are flavourful, and all the dishes are executed imaginitively. There are practiced hands in this kitchen. Lunch special dim sum (every day) is very popular. Rice ball desserts are a great way to end a meal.

Mr. Wu opened Gourmet Vegetarian Restaurant in September 2001. It was an immediate hit in this Chinese neighbourhood. This is a possible date place with tablecloths and modest decoration. It seats about 100 people, kids are welcome, and you can park in the mall. It's hard to beat tasty Chinese food that's also good for you—and not have a problem parking too!

Grano

2035 Yonge St. (bet. Davisville & Eglinton)
Subway: Eglinton or Davisville
Phone: 416.440.1986
Hours: Mon-Sat 10am-11pm; closed Sunday
Credit cards: V, MC, Amex, Diners; Alcohol: all
Wheelchair access: no
Antipasti: 3/$11.95, 5/$16.95; Pasta $12.95

The Italian antipasto and pasta dishes at Grano in the Yonge-Davisville area are a great deal!

The antipasti are an amazing signature feature. They're a large and tantalizing array displayed in a long deli cooler display case—and they taste even better than they look. The 3-plate selection makes a fine light meal, or you can share more with a group. Choices include vegetarian, seafood and meat selections. Try the artichokes, mushrooms, green beans, roasted peppers, and seasoned cubed potato. House-made daily soups are hearty and combine well to make a wonderful meal deal. The salad is the stuff of dreams and cravings: arugula with goat cheese crostini and pear slices in a dressing with figs, mustard, and olive oil. Excellent pasta or the creamy daily risotto comes in half or full portions. The orecchiette della nonna are a fine tumble of rapini, smoked prosciutto, sundried tomato purée, garlic, and olive oil in a white wine sauce. (Lucky you if you have a nonna who cooks like this!). The meat and seafood main courses will take you over the *Cheap Thrills* limit, but there are many other choices available and they're all good.

Grano has been around since the mid 80s serving reasonably priced quality food that is as fresh and delicious as ever. This is a welcoming place, bustling and casual, distinctly uptown North Toronto stylish, with a comfortable décor. It's terrific for a twosome, or for groups, families, and kids. Grano offers great value for contemporary Italian cooking with traditional references!

Greek Odyssey Souvlaki & Grill

1415 Kennedy Rd. (at Ellesmere)
Subway: Kennedy
Phone: 416.750.0010
Hours: Sun-Thur 11am-1am; until 2 am Fri & Sat
Credit cards: V, MC, Amex; Alcohol: all
Wheelchair access: yes
Average main course: $10

Eating at Greek Odyssey is a friendly and delicious experience either inside or in their Scarborough landmark outdoor tent.

The menu is extensive, including all the expected Greek specialties. The most popular main dishes are the chicken souvlaki in its various forms. The gyro (beef) and pork souvlaki are just as tender and perfectly grilled as the chicken. Most of the dinners are served withGreek salad, tzatziki, garlic bread, steamed fresh (not frozen) vegetables, and seriously good home-style roast lemon potatoes. The fried calamari appetizer is light and crisp. This is a great place to go with a crowd to share a a bunch of appetizers and main dishes. They also have moussaka, grilled fish, and seafood, although the latter can go beyond the *Cheap Thrills* guidelines. Everything is made in-house except the Serano Bakery baklava and Laroca's cheesecake or caramel crunch.

Chris and Soula Christodoulou and Mark Ghariba own and manage Greek Odyssey and they are very hands-on. This is not cookie-cutter fast food—they're masters of the grill! Chris started Mr. Greek on the Danforth with 15 seats in 1979, progressing to The Friendly Greek in 1989. When he sold out the name he decided to stay as an independent operation on Kennedy Road where they have been for seven years. Eating at Greek Odyssey is always pleasant and you can count on quality food and good service. They're busy so it's best to reserve ahead. The outdoor tent (heated as necessary) is available May through October and is particularly fun for families and groups.

Green Mango

730 Yonge St. (at Bloor)
Subway: Bloor
Phone: 416.928.0021
Hours: Mon-Sat 11am-10pm; Sun noon-9pm
Credit cards: cash only; Alcohol: no
Wheelchair access: yes
3006 Bloor St. W. (at Royal York)
Subway: Royal York
Phone: 416.233.5004
Credit cards: V, MC, Amex, Interac; Alcohol: beer & wine
Average main course: $5.95 combo plate

Green Mango serves dynamite Thai food in a quick spot at Yonge/Bloor and a fancier dining spot in Kingsway Village.

At the Bloor location you can choose from food that is already prepared or made to order. There's very high volume so even the popular ready-made is fresh. These choices tend to be mild/medium rather than spicy variations of noodles, vegetable dishes, tofu and chicken. The eggplant and tofu in basil sauce and the creamy vegetarian curry in coconut milk sauce are especially good. Combo plates include cabbage salad and great garnishes. Chicken lemongrass soup brings undiluted pleasure and comfort! You indicate your preferred level of spice for the made-to-order dishes, and they only take a few minutes extra. The pad Thai is a scrumptious symphony of taste and texture. Spring rolls are tightly-wrapped, crisp and tasty morsels. Chicken satay makes a fabulous quick snack at $2 a stick. No pork is served.

Green Mango has been delighting Torontonians since the early 1990s. They outgrew the original location at 707 Yonge—it's now Green Mango Soup Stories serving terrific Pan-Asian soups. The main location at 730 Yonge is well organized for efficient no-fuss eating or for a more leisurely meal. The Royal York location in the Kingsway Village offers a more pampered dining room with more delicate preparation, excellent service, and liquor license. All three operations are extremely well run and efficient with talented kitchen staff. Any one of the Green Mangos offers affordable, savoury, and authentic Thai!

Groucho's

1574 Bayview Ave. (at Eglinton)
Subway: Davisville
Phone: 416.482.3456
Hours: Mon-Sun 10:30am-10pm
Credit cards: Interac only; Alcohol: beer & wine
Wheelchair access: entrance yes; restroom no
994 Eglinton Ave. W. (at Allen Rd.)
Subway: Eglinton, then Eglinton bus west
Phone: 416.784.4434
Hours: Mon-Sun 10:30am-9pm
Credit cards: Interac only; Alcohol: no
Wheelchair access: yes
Burger combo: $5.95

Groucho's is a friendly neighbourhood burger joint in two North Toronto locations.

Groucho's is for burgers. They're big (6 oz.), juicy, nicely-grilled, with a good beefy taste. The cheeseburgers are made with real cheese (Swiss or cheddar)—no plastic. There is a huge and generous array of free burger toppings (all the regulars plus sauerkraut, tzatziki, cucumber) and for only a quarter each, gourmet toppings such as grilled eggplant or zucchini, artichoke hearts, roasted garlic or peppers, and guacamole. You can really load up and still not spend a fortune. They also have Caesar salad, veggie burgers, falafel burgers, and grilled chicken burgers. Delicious fresh cut fries and onion rings are fried in vegetable oil. Good kids' choices, include hot dogs and scrumptious grilled cheese sandwiches. Head elsewhere for dessert— at the Bayview branch there's a terrific gelato/sherbet place down the street.

Original owner Steve Lipsky sold Groucho's in 2001 to longtime employee Srikanthan Nadarajah. There's a portrait of Groucho, Steve's classic English bulldog, and lots of doggie memorabilia including a large doghouse trash/recycling bin. Dinner is served on trays and baskets and it's all deliciously finger food. Staff is young and friendly, and service is fast. There's a frequent diner card so the tenth burger is on the house. This is a very kid-friendly spot. Groucho's is a homey burger hangout with lots of choice, and they do take-out too.

Hair of the Dog

425 Church Street (cor. Wood St.)
Subway: College
Phone: 416.964.2708
Hours: Mon-Fri 11:30-2am; Sat, Sun & holidays 10-2am
Credit cards: V, MC, Diners, Interac; Alcohol: all
Wheelchair access: no
Average main course: $11

Hair of the Dog is a neighbourhood pub with an eclectic menu, generous portions, and reasonable prices in a former steak house near the old Maple Leaf Gardens at the foot of the Gay Village.

The menu is all over the map, so it fills the bill for a crowd with varied tastes or when you aren't too sure what kind of food you want to eat. They have Cajun, English pub food, Italian dishes, some Asian twists, burgers, pastas, and a pricier steak menu if you want to go beyond the *Cheap Thrills* parameters. A somewhat postmodern kitchen somehow makes it all work and miraculously all the food is excellent. Monday is pasta night, Tuesday is comfort food, and Wednesday is vegetarian. A favourite is the Cajun chicken salad—grilled chicken breast with fresh greens and a terrific sun-dried tomato vinaigrette. Some of the best bets are eggplant fusili, lasagne, meat or vegetarian burgers, banana curry penne, and jerk catfish. Weekend brunch includes a melty breakfast quesadilla. They have a decent selection of wine by the glass and specialty beers.

Michael Schwarz and Keir Macrae are the hosts in a casual, warm, bustling but mellow pub atmosphere with wonderful photo portraits of dogs on the walls. The dog photos alone are worth the trip! The upstairs room is quieter. LeBaron Steakhouse was in this space for many years but the neighbourhood is in transition since the Maple Leafs left the Gardens. They have a very pleasant patio. It's very easy to become a regular!

Hong Fatt

447 Dundas St. W. (at Huron)
Subway: St. Patrick, or Dundas streetcar
Phone: 416.977.3945
Hours: Mon-Sun 10am-10pm
Credit cards: cash only; Alcohol: no
Wheelchair access: no
Average main course: $7

Hong Fatt is a tiny hole-in-the-wall in Chinatown where you can get spectacular BBQ pork and duck.

The menu includes a whole raft of standard things that are completely acceptable, but the main attraction here are wondrous BBQ (and roast) pork and duck. A good soup comes without charge with BBQ meals. Then there's the BBQ—sumptuous morsels of moist rich brown pork ribs, or duck beautifully prepared and spiced, slow-cooked with meat that is juicy, tender and truly succulent. THIS IS GOOD STUFF—really good stuff. You'll fight your friends for the last bite!

Mrs. Lem has run Hong Fatt on Dundas, its second location, since 1958. This is a basic Chinese diner at its most genuine, with neon lights, yellow tables, and no ambiance or atmosphere except for the barbecued ducks hanging in the window and the cook who cuts them up in plain view. The surrounding streets have enough atmosphere to spare—the wonderful and diverse chaos of Toronto's Chinatown. They go through two whole hogs a day! There are big round tables and the service is fast, but they do mostly take-out. You can get dessert at the fortune cookie factory across the street. Hong Fatt has no pretension, no pretty public face. They just do what they do and do it very, very well. Get here. Eat the BBQ. You'll be glad you did!

Ho Su Bistro

254 Queen St. W. (at John St.)
Subway: Osgoode; or Queen West streetcar
Phone: 416.848.9456
Hours: Sun-Thur 11:30am-10pm; Fri & Sat 11:30am-midnight
Credit cards: V, MC, Amex, Diners, Interac; Alcohol: all
Wheelchair access: entrance yes; restroom no
2352 Yonge St. (at Eglinton)
Subway: Eglinton
Phone: 416.322.6860
Wheelchair access: no
Average main course: $8.95

Ho Su Bistro specializes in Korean and Japanese food at two locations—Queen West and Yonge & Eglinton.

The house specialties are superbly done tempura dishes, wonderfully-fresh sushi, and bi bim bop, the signature Korean dish. The tempura jumbo shrimp are a jumbo delight—over five inches long with a light crunchy batter, delicate flavour, and just the right dash of sea salt. The same batter is on the generous calamari appetizer. The dipping sauce is awesome, warmed soy sauce with a little sugar, and a light caramel flavour. There are interesting vegetarian options like potato tempura, vegetarian maki, stir-fried buckwheat noodles, and even a vegetarian bento box. Tempura veggies include potato, zucchini, broccoli, and sweet potato—a wonderful excuse for the dipping sauce. The Sushi Bar produces a super-fresh rendition of a California roll, and the warmed wasabi/soy sauce dipping sauce ratchets it up several notches, creating layers of sweet and super-spicy. Delicious bi bim bop—meat or vegetables with steamed rice—is served in a stone bowl. There are daily specials and the always-elegant and varied bento boxes. Both include a salad with a deliriously good dressing! Sushi sampler or Korean chicken will not fail to please. Lunch specials are available.

The Sushi Bar is front and centre as you enter the restaurant. The three dining rooms are quiet and calming, with recessed lighting, high ceilings, and very comfortable chairs. Things can get a little slow when they're busy but staff are friendly and helpful.

Island Foods

109 McCaul St. (bet. Dundas & Queen)
Subway: St. Patrick, or Queen streetcar
Phone: 416.599.9339
Hours: Mon-Fri 11am-8:30pm
Credit cards: V, MC, Amex, Interac; Alcohol: no
Wheelchair access: yes
1182 King St. W. (at Dufferin)
Subway: St. Andrew, then the King streetcar west
Phone: 416.532.6298
Hours: Mon-Sat 11am-9:30pm
Credit cards: V, Amex, Interac; Alcohol: all
Wheelchair access: yes
Average main course: $6.50

Island Foods serves wonderful Trinidad-style rotis and other West Indian specialties in Village By the Grange (near the AGO) and on King Street at Dufferin.

Complex and flavourful hot sauce is available mild, medium, and seriously hot. Rotis are really delectable! Fillings are wonderful curry-scented mixtures of cabbage, cauliflower, green peppers and shrimp, boneless chicken or goat, beef, chickpeas, eggplant, potato or dhalpouri. They're packed with flavour, moist and delicious. The chickpea and the potato are real favourites. They also have dinners served with curry potatoes, rice and peas—jerk chicken is popular, goat curry has rich and tasty gravy, and the vegetarian is incredibly good. Great snacks are tamarind balls or stupendously good doubles—chickpea curry between two puffy seasoned pancakes (alas, not always available at peak times). Tropical juices (especially Grace grapefruit) pair well with the food.

The Sawh family started Island Foods in 1974 at Dufferin Mall and the family still runs it. They opened on King in 1986, moved from the original location at Dufferin Mall to the south end of Village By the Grange in 1999, and they've been at the CNE every year since 1976. These are not luxurious or fancy locations but they're relaxed and pleasant enough, and they do a big takeout business. Staff are friendly and approachable. This is really good food from Trinidad, and the hot sauces are the perfect accompaniment.

Izmi Sushi Japanese Restaurant

714 Queen St. W. (Bet. Manning & Claremont)
Subway: Bathurst, then Bathurst streetcar south
Phone: 416.361.6355
Hours: 11:30am-10pm
Credit cards: V, MC, Amex, Interac; Alcohol: all
Wheelchair access: yes
Average main course: $10.50

Izmi is a low-key sushi-and-more place on Queen West that serves quality Japanese food at unforgettable prices.

You can eat sushi or a selection of other Japanese food here—all of it excellent! Great Izmi is arguably the best tempura deal in Toronto. It's light and crispy and the portions are indeed "great" with seven large shrimp and a generous array of vegetable tempura, all served with rice, salad and soup—for only $14.95. Vegetarian tempura is also excellent. The main draw is the sushi—portions are generous and offer wonderful value. It's fresh and done right. The *take* sushi combo includes 8 pieces, soup and salad for only $12.95. There's even a special bento lunch deal. The deep fried soft shell crab is delightful, and the chicken or beef teriyaki are reliable standbys. The kitchen is MSG-free. They do catering and take-out.

Izmi opened in July 2001. The interior décor is modern Japanese minimalist once you get beyond the neon front window and doorway. Uncluttered almost to a fault, there's an open, roomy ambiance, and it's bright and pleasant. The sushi bar is comfortable. Staff are attentive and pleasant although English is clearly not their first language. Affordable quality Japanese food, let alone sushi, is almost an oxymoron so rush over to Izmi before the prices change!

Jawny Bakers

804 O'Connor Drive (cor. St. Clair Ave.), East York
Bus: 91 from Woodbine subway station; or 70/71A from Coxwell
    subway station
Phone: 416.285.1165
Hours: Mon-Sat 11am-1am; Sun 11am-10pm
Credit cards: V, MC, Amex; Alcohol: all
Wheelchair access: yes
Average main course: $9.50

Jawny Bakers is a Down Home Southwest style place near Woodbine that serves good burgers, pizzas, pastas, with a cake and ice cream finish.

You can order a variety of burgers, pizzas (thin crust), pastas, and hot sandwiches. They have a pizza, sandwich, and blue plate of the day and these are always a good deal. Steak and seafood specialties will take you over the *Cheap Thrills* limit, but the wing/rib combo is a real treat. There is a homemade soup every day, and the Cajun chicken club sandwich is a real winner, as is the Mediterranean salad. Wednesday is wings night, Thursday is Mexican, and Sunday is kids night. The fries are fresh cut and fried in vegetable oil. Meats are char-grilled and there is a healthy touch to it all rather than indulgent and greasy old-style comfort food. Everything is fresh and nicely presented. There's a special menu for kids ten and under ($4.99). Best of all there are wonderful cakes or pies and ice cream for dessert from Laroca or Honeycrust Bakeries!

Jawny Bakers opened in 1992, and is still owned by the Zoras family (brother, sister, and cousin) and it's warm and inviting with wooden floors, an open fireplace, wooden tables, and booths. There is a bar to the side (where you can eat and smoke too) if you don't want to mingle with family diners. This is a neighbourhood hangout for all and sundry, friendly and not at all pretentious but with a pleasant and engaging atmosphere and good food. When did you last indulge in cake and ice cream for dessert?

Jean's Fine Foods Catering

2326 Danforth Ave. (bet. Woodbine Ave. & Main St.)
Subway: Woodbine
Phone: 416.422.0617
Hours: Tue-Sun 5pm-10pm; closed Monday
Credit cards: V, MC, Interac; Alcohol: no
Wheelchair access: entrance yes; restroom no
Average main course: $8

Jean's Fine Foods on Danforth near Woodbine offers delectable Thai and Malaysian food made with tender loving care.

You can choose from Thai staples like pad Thai, BBQ or satay chicken, and fishcakes. Or try Malaysian noodles, chicken curry, rendang beef or chicken, or sambal pork or seafood. Everything here is good! Food is prepared fresh with lots of basil, coconut, and lemongrass, and there is an experienced and accomplished authenticity to each and every dish. This kitchen knows what it is doing. Flavourings never overpower but always add interesting layers to the natural flavours of good basic ingredients. All curry pastes and spices are blended in-house and the freshness and quality are evident throughout. There is a good selection of vegetarian dishes. You can request your preferred level of hotness, or you can add extra hot sauce at the table. This is a menu you will want to explore thoroughly.

Jean and Harry Seow are the chef-owners who began Jean's Fine Foods as a retirement project. He is a trained Malay chef and she is a Thai chef. The quality and authenticity of the food is striking! It's a friendly place, modestly decorated, where the quality of the food and Jean and Harry's contagious hospitality are the most important considerations. The neighbourhood has responded well to their warm and inviting ambiance. We're lucky they didn't choose to take up lawn bowling or needlepoint!

Jodhpore Club

33 Baldwin St. (at Henry St.)
Subway: Queen's Park, or College streetcar
Phone: 416.598.2502
Hours: Mon-Sun 11:30am-3pm & 5pm-10pm
Credit cards: V, MC, Amex; Alcohol: all
Wheelchair access: no
Average main course: $8

Jodhpore Club in the heart of Baldwin Village serves North Indian and Goan specialties.

House specials include tandoor salmon, beautifully-marinated in a fresh paste of mint, fenugreek, mustard and carum seeds from the legendary West Coast of India, then cooked slowly over coals. The delectable Pudhine lamb chop is Kabul-style (wrapped and cooked in its own steam), lightly marinated in yogurt and mint, then barbecued with herbs. Chicken Jalfrezi is boneless tandoor chicken sautéed with sweet peppers, onions, and tomatoes. Beef narangi is braised in a wonderful aromatic sauce of orange and spice. Seafood is done Goan-style with Portuguese-influenced fiery peppers and vinegar marinades. Veggies are prepared with a deft touch. The daily lunch buffet ($7) is fast and fabulous! Braised lamb shanks and prawns with mint, cilantro, chillies, and coconut are both winners. Their version of mango lassi is exquisite.

Jodhpore Club opened in 2001, named for the town of Jodhpore in northwest India, and famous for the very old game of polo that was popular in 19th century India, and adopted by the English. Owner-chef Jay Vaidya from New Delhi knows his stuff. He's a gifted chef who combines local ingredients with his knowledge of North Indian and Goan cooking styles. Everything is richly flavoured, artfully-spiced and designed for good eating. You won't find fancy décor but it's a pleasant place on a charming block, with warm copper touches and lots of ambiance. It's small so be sure to reserve! Jodhpore Club turns out consistently terrific food that's great bang for your buck!

John's Classic Italian Pizza

591 College St. (at Clinton)
Streetcar: College
Phone: 416.537.2794; delivery 416.537.0598
Hours: Mon-Sun noon-10pm
Credit cards: V, MC; Alcohol: beer
Wheelchair access: no
Average main course: $7.50

John's Classic Italian Pizza serves wonderful thin-crust pizza in Little Italy.

The menu includes flawlessly executed home-style classics like lasagne, penne with sausage, bubbling hot, cheesy fusilli baked in the oven, and pasta and salads too. But really, pizza reigns here. It's available by the slice (from a changing selection of about 5) or by the pie. The slices are large and two are enough for a meal, or a 14-inch pizza made to order serves two hungry people. You can go up to 18 inches for more people or if you've been on a starvation regime for a month or so. You can get all the usual toppings plus grilled eggplant, roasted or jalapeno peppers, goat cheese, gorgonzola, smoked provolone, seafood, and other goodies. One of the best and most popular pizzas is with mozzarella, spinach, sun-dried tomatoes, goat cheese and pesto. It's a great combo with Creemore or Steamwhistle on tap, or with Brio! The coffee is smooth and mellow.

John's is not the place to go for a refined dining experience, but it's comfortable and relaxed, and the décor is authentic pizza bar. They do a significant take-out and delivery business, and they DO have a window on one of the trendiest corners of College Street—perfect for people watching.

Juice for Life

521 Bloor St. W. (at Borden St.)
Subway: Bathurst
Phone: 416.531.2635
Hours: Mon-Fri 11:30am-10pm; Sat & Sun 10:30am-10pm
Credit cards: V, MC, Amex, Interac; Alcohol: beer & wine
Wheelchair access: no
336 Queen St. W. (at Spadina)
Streetcar: Queen streetcar, or Spadina bus
Phone: 416.599.4442
Hours: Mon-Fri 8:30am-6pm; Sat & Sun 9am-6pm
Credit cards: V, MC, Amex, Interac; Alcohol: no
Wheelchair access: entrance yes; restroom no
Average main course: $8.95

Juice for Life is a vegetarian haven for gourmet health food and juices.

The menu is a healthy and appealing vegetarian menu without hidden meat, dairy or egg products of any kind. An extensive selection of juices and power shakes have wonderful combinations of fresh fruit and vegetables and added goodies like organic hulled hemp, ginseng, royal jelly, soy protein, wheatgrass, spirulina, etc. Organic yogourt or rice milk is optional. There are also smoothies and lassis, organic Fair Trade espresso, and spiced chai. You feel virtuous just reading the menu! Main courses include wonderful salads with great dressings, fabulous rice bowls, noodles, as well as veggie burgers and sandwiches. Fries are fresh and delectable, a favourite served with herbs and other yummy toppings.

Ruth Tal Brown began Juice for Life in 1994 as an expansion of her travelling juice cart. The hip Queen Street location is the original juice bar and it offers counter service and take-out only. Bloor in the Annex is a full-service restaurant and a third location is planned for Queen and Crawford in summer 2002. Clientele and staff tend to be young and it's all very friendly with plenty of celebrity visitors and energized diners. The crowd and the juicers make for a noisy back-ground but it all seems to come together very nicely anyway. This is a popular and engaging vegetarian hangout.

Julie's Cuban Snack Bar

202 Dovercourt Rd. (at Foxley St.)
Streetcar: Queen or Dundas streetcar
Phone: 416.532.7397
Hours: Tue-Fri 6pm-2am; Sat & Sun 11:30am-2am
Credit cards: V, MC; Alcohol: all
Wheelchair access: no
Average tapas: $6

Julie's Snack Bar serves Cuban food and sensational *mojitos* in the Dovercourt Park area.

The menu is a mix of small dishes (*aperitivos/tapas*) and main dishes. The mains tend to be more expensive and some fall outside the Cheap *Thrills* guidelines. The slightly spicey *picadillo de Mamita* (beef and pork with saffron rice) is flavourful home cooking at its best. It's a good idea to check out their daily specials, but the big attraction here is the *tapas*. There is a fabulous selection that includes ceviche, shrimp, squid, chorizo, wonderful fried plantains, outstanding corn fritters, and an excellent potato puff. The best way to go is to order a selection of things and share. Don't expect lots of fresh green veggies or haute cuisine—this is basic food cooked Cuban style. Ah, but then there are the rum-mint *mojitos*! (not to mention a raft of other fabulous tropical drinks) They will see you through a hot summer day or the winter doldrums—they may be the best in town!

Julie's Snack Bar was run by Julie Berezansky as a local eatery for 30 years until the early 90s. It was reincarnated in 1995 when Julie's daughter Sylvia Llewellyn and Cuban partner Jesús Baute started serving Cuban specialties. This is a comfortable and comforting neighbourhood place where the living is easy and everyone is friendly and helpful. They are on a tree-lined street with a terrific patio where you can sit with your *mojito* and some *tapas* to while away an afternoon or evening!

Jumbo Empanadas

245 Augusta Ave. (in Kensington Market)
Subway: Queen's Park, then College streetcar; or Spadina
    streetcar
Phone: 416.977.0056
Hours: Mon-Sat 9am-8pm; Sun 11am-5pm
Credit cards: cash only; Alcohol: no
Wheelchair access: no
Empanaadas or humitas: $3.50

You can get really good Chilean street-style food at Jumbo
Empanadas in Kensington Market.

The menu is posted on the wall. The main event are the
empanadas—beef, chicken, and vegetable. They're made on
site with good pastry and they are generous and nicely stuffed,
including the requisite slice of boiled egg and a black olive.
The vegetarian version has a fusion twist with pesto, fried
spinach, onion, mushroom, and red pepper. The house salsa
is a zesty, but relatively tame, mix of tomato, cilantro, garlic
and onion and it complements the empanadas and other
foods beautifully. The *humitas* are delicious tamale-like
dumplings—careful they run out of these early in the day.
The *pastel de chocio* (sweet corn pie) is a delicious shepherd's
pie-like concoction with a layer of browned mashed sweet
corn over a layer of beef, chicken, olives and raisins, nicely
combining sweet and savoury. Saturday specials are homemade buns and *sopaipillas*, delicious squash tortillas sprinkled
with sugar. They have a nice selection of Latin American fruit
drinks and sodas.

Owner Irene Morales, originally from Chile, started making
empanadas from her mother's recipes and selling them from
a pushcart in the Market in 1988. By 1994 she opened the
café that she now runs with her daughter Lily—a real success
story! They make 400 empanadas a day in winter, and many
more in summer. They are friendly and helpful and you can
practice your Spanish. It's a modest and informal space with
an open terrace front, an open kitchen, AND really good food!

Kensington Kitchen

124 Harbord St. (at Spadina)
Subway: Spadina, or Harbord bus
Phone: 416.961.3404
Hours: Sun-Thur 11am-10pm; Fri & Sat until 10:30pm
Credit cards: V, MC, Amex, Diners; Alcohol: all
Wheelchair access: no
Average main course: $12

Kensington Kitchen is a delightful café in the Annex with stylish Mediterranean food.

The menu does a cook's tour of the Mediterranean. The antipasti platter has a bit of everything. It's a meal in itself or it can be paired with other choices for a group banquet. *Farfalle* (bows) with pesto and optional chicken or spicy Italian sausage is delightful and satisfying. Moroccan couscous (with or without optional meat or seafood) is savoury North African comfort food. For a deliriously indulgent treat share a heap of fries made with Yukon Gold potatoes and served with garlic aioli. Yes, it's gilding the lily, but what gilding and what a lily! Calamari with aioli and harissa is first-rate. The "lamburger" is a huge, tasty, juicy, slightly pink lamb patty dressed with tomato and feta, and served with creamy, garlicky Caesar salad—mmmm! Istanbul lamb is a sweet and savoury wonder. Some of the main courses would take you beyond the *Cheap Thrills* guidelines but portions are large so sharing is a real option. Coffee is excellent.

Kensington Kitchen opened near the Kensington Market in 1981, but it's been in the Annex for a long time. Anwar (see sPaHa) has joined his dad, original owner Said Mukhayesh, and the talented chef is Abdellatif Belkadi. They all pay attention to the food and keep the menu evolving. The rooftop patio is a very special tree house retreat but indoors is also very agreeable. Service, atmosphere, and food are polished but the whole show is very hip and friendly. You can do a blowout Mediterranean feast here but you can also do well on a budget.

Kom Jug Yuen

371 Spadina Ave (at Cecil)
Subway: Queen's Park or Spadina
Phone: 416.977.4079
Hours: Mon, Wed, Thur, Sun 11am-1am; Tues 11am-11pm;
    until 4 am Fri & Sat
Credit cards: V, MC, Interac; Alcohol: no
Wheelchair access: no
Average main course: $7

Kom Jug Yuen serves fresh Chinese food at really low prices in an unassuming space in Chinatown.

One of the house specialties is the crispy beef, a real salt hit but truly outstanding and addictive. Thin deep-fried crispy rounds of salty beef are served with a spicy sauce. Noodle dishes are spicy, with the curried Singapore vermicelli a special treat of shrimp and vegetables made fresh every time and served steaming hot. Pickerel in black bean sauce is also excellent. BBQ pork, duck and ribs are done nicely, with a big portion for a small price. The duck is moist with an intense and smoky taste. There are specials featuring food that is not haute cuisine but fresh and honest, not soggy or dried out after sitting for hours on a steam table.

Kom Jug Yuen has been around for about 20 years and it is very well known in the Chinese community as a place to get decent food at indecent prices. It's a bit of a dive, and the atmosphere and ambiance leave a lot to be desired but there's always takeout. They're open very late on weekends so it's a perfect destination after a night out on the town. The bonus is that for a Toronto Chinese restaurant the service is fast, friendly and courteous—the staff even smile! Kom Jug Yuen is a great place for those who want to eat well on a very tight budget!

Kon-nichi-wa Deli

31 Baldwin St. (at Henry St.)
Subway: St. Patrick, or College streetcar
Phone: 416.593.8538
Hours: Mon-Sat 11:30am-10pm; closed Sunday
Credit cards: V, Interac; Alcohol: beer & sake
Wheelchair acccess: no
Average main course: $6

Japanese noodles and home-style cooking is available at Kon-nichi-wa Deli on Baldwin Street near the AGO.

Noodles are a real treat here. The soups are made with a marvellous secret-recipe stock and you can choose wheat noodles (udon) or buckwheat (soba). The broth is traditional, fashioned so you actually taste the noodles in all their goodness. The noodles come paired with beef, chicken, tofu, shrimp, and vegetable or mixed tempura. They also serve *tampopo* ramen with pork and veggies. All are absolutely delicious, cleansing, and life-sustaining. They feel like ancient health food. The teriyaki with chicken, beef or tofu, and the tempuras are Japanese staples that are done beautifully here. They also serve donburi, rice with breaded cutlets (pork, chicken, beef, tofu) or veggie tempura. The kitchen also produces a small selection of fresh and delicious shrimp and vegetarian sushi.

The charming Sonoe Howard (with help from her sister Shizuko) from southern Japan has owned and operated this modest but gracious dining space since 1996. They've been doing real Japanese food in Toronto since they opened Mariko in 1984 (now sold). The food at Kon-nichi-wa (which means hello) is truly authentic from family recipes, with virtually everything made from scratch. The food is light, lean, and less salty than you might find in Japan but otherwise it's the real thing. There's a pleasant patio on Baldwin—great for people watching. Service is good on all counts. Kon-nichi-wa serves authentic, simple, and quality Japanese noodles and other home cooking on trendy Baldwin Street.

Lahore Tikka House

1365 Gerrard St. E. (2 blocks E. of Greenwood)
Streetcar: #506Carlton streetcar; or #31 Greenwood bus
Phone: 416.406.1668
Hours: Mon-Thur & Sun noon-midnight; Fri & Sat noon-1am
Credit cards: V, MC, Amex, Interac; Alcohol: no
Wheelchair access: entrance yes; restroom no
Average main course: $7.50

Lahore Tikka House is the place to go for really good halal Pakistani food, with no smoking or alcohol, and a large patio on the Indian strip on Gerrard East.

The tandoori chicken is tender with crusted BBQ edges, served with plenty of rice, tandoori roasted whole chili pepper and onions, and a green salad with yogurt dressing. Biranyis are also terrific. Kebabs are cooked perfectly and are available individually or as part of a larger plate. The chicken *tikka masala* is a winner, and there are vegetarian choices available. Wonderful samosas will set you back only 99 cents, and the nan ($1) is made as you watch on the patio in summer. All portions are generous and sharing is highly recommended unless you want doggie bags. They use halal meat so that's an extra layer of quality control.

Lahore Tikka House has been around since the early 1990s in a small storefront. They expanded to the current larger space and will expand again sometime soon, but plan to keep the same atmosphere. The décor is minimal but there's a neighbourhood feeling, and the focus is on the food. You place your order at the counter, take a number, and the food is brought to you when it's ready. It's all very friendly and casual but efficient. In good weather much of the cooking is done outside, to the delight of diners. There's a substantial take-out business. Kids are welcome and feel right at home. This is THE place to come for a home-style meal after shopping nearby for sari fabrics, music, and foodstuffs.

Liberty Street Café

25 Liberty St. (at Atlantic St.)
Subway: St. Andrew; then 504 King streetcar
Phone: 416.533.8828
Hours: Mon-Thur noon-midnight; until 1am Fri;
 Sat 11am-1am; until midnight Sun
Credit cards: V, MC, Amex, Interac; Alcohol: all
Wheelchair access: no
Average main course: $8

The Liberty Street Café patio is a great spot for summer outdoor eating with live jazz on weekends, and a great view of the Toronto skyline near King and Dufferin.

The food is pub style rather than gourmet. The menu ranges wide and includes salads, pizza, pasta, sandwiches, rotisserie chicken, and other main courses. The time-tested favourites are the weekend brunch specials, pizza, rotisserie chicken, and the Liberty burger. Rotisserie chicken is an excellent choice, perfectly cooked, juicy and tasty. The Philly sandwich is also popular. The burgers are a full eight ounces of beef perfectly cooked to order; peameal bacon is optional, as are extra toppings of a variety of cheeses or veggies. Do yourself a favour and pass on the fries in favour of a beer. The blue nachos come with tasty guacamole, sour cream, and meat chilli as a nice added touch. Stuffed jalapeños are plump with cream cheese. The beer-basted Brazilian-style back ribs are messy but great.

Liberty Street Café is technically a bar so even though it's spacious, it can get smoky and no kids are allowed. It's been around since 1990 but Michael Cabral bought it only in December 2001 and he's done a facelift of the space and the menu. People from nearby movie studios and design firms are lunchtime regulars but the patio is a big draw for balmy summer evenings. Staff are friendly and helpful. You'll fantasize all winter about having a good burger and a cold pint on the wonderful ivy-covered patio listening to live jazz.

Lick's Homeburgers & Ice Cream

860 York Mills Rd. (at Lesmill Road), North York
49 Eglinton Ave. E. (at Yonge)
1960 Queen St. E. (at Woodbine)
285 Rexdale Blvd. (at Martingrove)
plus 20 other locations in the GTA
For hours and locations, visit: *www.lickshomeburgers.com*
or call 416.362.LICKS (5425)
Average combo meal: $5.99

Lick's is a high-quality hamburger place and ice cream parlour, a small Toronto chain that offers good food and a good deal.

Cheap Thrills does not include fast-food chain restaurants, but we've made an exception for this Toronto institution. The burgers are pasteurized lean ground steak, thick and juicy, charcoal broiled on a real grill. There are about 15 toppings including alfalfa sprouts, cucumber slices, and Guk, Lick's special spicy mayo. The menu includes the homeburger, 6 ounces of beef, the gobbler (ground turkey), Chick'n Lick'n and Chick'n Club (moist and tender chicken), and the vegetarian nature burger. Add an extra patty for $2. Their ice cream is yummy. Lick's shakes are made with scoops of real ice cream or frozen yogurt, always thick, creamy and natural. Cones (regular or waffle), banana splits and sundaes are large, with many topping options.

Lick's is a Canadian owned and operated chain of 24 Toronto-area restaurants that Denise Meehan started as an ice cream store. It's been a storybook success story with consistent quality and service and many loyal fans. The restaurants are all different with an ice cream parlour atmosphere. Seating is comfortable, but the set-up is basic, not luxurious. You place your order at the cash and then you choose your toppings and condiments. There's a special kid's menu and some branches have a play area. Staff is young, courteous, and friendly and they sometimes break into song! None of the burgers taste pre-packaged. Lick's reliably provides fast food with a fresh and tasty twist.

The Living Well Café

692 Yonge St. (at St. Mary)
Subway: Bloor
Phone: 416.922.6770
Hours: Mon-Sun 11:30am-1am; lounge upstairs 6pm-2am
Credit cards: V, MC, Amex, Interac; Alcohol: all
Wheelchair access: no
Average main course: $10

The Living Well Café, a late-night eatery and bar in the heart of the gay community, near Yonge and Bloor, serves eclectic bistro food seven days a week.

There's a little bit of everything on this menu, and daily blackboard specials too. They have everything from delicious classic onion soup to a lovely version of trendy raspberry chicken, pasta, burgers (juicy 8 ounces!), and Asian-influenced dishes. Louisiana raspberry chicken is a favourite, with Cajun spices, savoury sauce, and sides of pasta Alfredo and Cajun corn. Pad Thai is a fragrant tumble of taste and texture with tiger shrimp, chicken breast, noodles, fresh basil and coriander. There's a wide selection of vegetarian dishes. Weekend brunch runs from 11:30 am to 3 pm and you can indulge in eggs Florentine or sinfully decadent eggs Benedict. Combo plates and lunch specials are a wonderful inexpensive way to while away a lunchtime break. Go upstairs Monday night for benefit Dirty Bingo with Shirley or Thursday for Martini Madness.

Owner Dino Magnatta opened a small vegetarian café here in 1981, and it's grown into an inviting place with casual, downtown chic and a varied menu of first-rate food. Chef Kumar Balendra knows his way around the kitchen. There are two secluded back patios, photos on the walls, a gothic chandelier, and an upstairs lounge. The noise level is reasonable although it gets crowded, and there's smoking in the back. "Living Well is the Best Revenge"—it's fun and funky with something for everyone!

Magic Oven

788 Broadview Ave. (at Danforth)
Subway: Broadview
Phone: 416.466.0111
Hours: Mon-Fri 4pm-11pm; Sat & Sun 4pm-10pm
Credit cards: V, MC, Amex, Interac; Alcohol: no
Wheelchair access: no
Average main course: $9

Magic Oven is an upscale Riverdale pizzeria that also serves pasta, salads, and sandwiches, with a nod to health-conscious options.

The quality of the food is a notch above the average pizzeria. Ingredients are high quality and the combinations are innovative and interesting. In addition to regular offerings they make gluten-free pasta or pizza and organic spelt pizza crusts. The chicken is free-range, there are no preservatives or MSG, and there are vegan options. Really fine pizzas are at the centre of the menu. Salads are super fresh and beautifully dressed. One of the house specialties is Tandoori magic, a vegetarian tandoori potato pizza, probably the only one of its kind in the world. The delectable chicken pesto magic pizza combines Thai chicken, basil and goat cheese. The super best bet here is the Combo Special: a specialty pizza, a large salad, garlic bread, and 2 litres of Pepsi for eat-in or take-out—more than enough for two!

Tony Sabherwal has owned Magic Oven since 1996, and he makes changes to the menu a couple of times a year, responding to customer feedback. This area is increasingly young, hip and health-conscious, so Magic Oven leans towards good-tasting vegetarian and vegan options with different cheeses and fresh herbs. They do a brisk catering and take-out business. This is a small, friendly, and functional but comfortable place with a handful of tables and feel-good food.

Mamma's Pizza

405 Richmond St. W. (at Spadina)
Subway: Spadina, then Spadina bus; or Queen West streetcar
Phone: 416.598.8886
Hours: Mon-Wed 11am-midnight; until 1am Thur;
   until 3am Fri & Sat; Sun noon-midnight
Credit cards: V, MC, Amex, Interac; Alcohol: beer & wine
Wheelchair access: entrance yes; restroom no
Average main course: $7
807 Yonge St. (at Bloor)
Phone: 416.310.6266
Plus 8 other locations in Toronto. Go to *www.mammaspizza.com*

Mamma's Pizza does take-out, delivery, and eat-in of some of the finest pizza in Toronto, in several locations.

They offer pizza, calzones, sandwiches, and pastas, but the pizza really steals the show. Regulars claim it's the best traditional thin crust pizza place in town. They have minimal rise, but are fired just right so that you can eat the slices without utensils. They have perfect fresh-baked crunch and an olive oil finish that doesn't compromise the crust. The *pizza al pollo* is unusual but sensational with small pieces of marinated chicken, roasted red peppers and red onions. The toppings and combinations are extensive and include all the regulars and special goodies like grilled eggplant slices, capers, goat cheese, etc. They take particular care to make sure the spread is even so each bite has all the tastes.

Lidia Danesi emigrated from Tuscany and founded the Monte Carlo Restaurant in Toronto in 1957. She made pizza and eventually the name changed to Mamma's Pizza. The whole show is now being run by the second and third generations of the family in expanding locations. The Richmond Street location is in the Queen West and galleries neighbourhood and the Yonge Street branch is great for a break after a visit to the Toronto Reference Library. It's far from a standard fast-food chain and they've somehow still managed to maintain quality. All the food is Italian-mama-good, but it's hard to resist that pizza whether you think it ranks first, second or third!

Mars Restaurant

432 College St. (at Bathurst)
Subway: Bathurst, then Bathurst South streetcar
Phone: 416.921.6332
Hours: Sun-Wed 7am-7:30pm; until 9 pm Thur; open 24 hours
  Fri & Sat
Credit cards: V, MC, Amex, Interac; Alcohol: no
Wheelchair access: entrance yes; restroom no
Average main course: almost impossible to spend more than $10

Mars Restaurant serves all-day breakfast and homey lunch
and dinner food all day every day at a fifties-style diner on
College near Bathurst.

Breakfast Any Time is the star attraction—and this is
breakfast as it used to be! Eggs any style, fluffy omelettes,
salami, sausage, bacon, corn beef hash, cheese blintzes with
sour cream, griddle cakes, freshly squeezed orange juice,
white/brown/rye toast,muffins to die for, and even stewed
prunes! The time-tested corn, bran, and blueberry muffins
have helped generations face the morning. The specials offer
a number of Big Hungry combos, including the Mr. Mars
Special ($8.95) that offers 3 eggs, a 6-ounce steak, home fries,
toast and coffee. It's all cooked to order and done just as you
like it in full view. They also serve homemade soup, a great
burger, a nicely grilled pork chop, and all the standard sandwiches, including grilled cheese, chopped liver, tuna, ham and
tomato, and some massive three-deckers. Everything is
prepared simply but perfectly and without nouvelle twists.
Daily specials are never-fail! The turnover is high so all is
super-fresh. Everything is made the way your Great Aunt
Agnes would have done it.

Mars is not a retro snack bar, it's the real thing. It opened
in 1951 and has been owned and run by Steve Tsecaris since
1958, when getting to Mars was a wild dream. The logo on
the dishes says "Just out of this world." There's a long lunch
counter with stools, and booths at the back. This is a perfect
place to read your paper, chat with your neighbour if you
like, or just eat and run. Leave your cholesterol count at the
door and enjoy a little time warp back to the fifties. This place
is good for the soul!

Mezzetta Café Restaurant

681 St. Clair Ave. W. (at Christie)
Subway: St. Clair West
Phone: 416.658.5687
Hours: Tue-Fri noon-2:30pm & 5pm-11pm; until 11:30 pm Sat;
    Sun 5pm-10pm only
Credit cards: cash only; Alcohol: all
Wheelchair access: no
Every item $2.95 (except $2 Tuesday dinner)

Mezzetta serves a slew of scrumptious Middle Eastern tidbits on St. Clair West.

They serve only appetizers, small specialty dishes from the likes of Turkey, Lebanon, Morrocco, and Iran. They add up to make a complete meal here. They recommend 5 dishes per person for a full meal (and they discount in multiples of 5), but you can adjust to your own appetite level. Succulent Sultan's stew is an amazing and wonderful eggplant dish, Moroccan carrots are spicy and delicious with mint and chickpeas, and the marinated mushrooms are superb. There are also spicy green beans, tabouleh, wonderful kebabs (fish, chicken, or lamb), falafel, hummous, baba ganouj, beef-lamb sausages, home-smoked salmon, and delicious kofta beef balls in a savoury tomato sauce. Whatever you do, don't miss the amazing fried yams. There is quite a selection and it's all good! They use only vegetable oil for frying, and foods are dressed with extra-virgin olive oil.

Mezzetta has been around since 1991. Current owner Safa Nematy took over from the original Israeli owner in 1994, and he claims to live on eggplant so it's a favourite here and the eggplant dishes are good indeed! The variety is amazing and there's something for every palate—the whole menu is a journey of discovery as you try a few new dishes each time. The décor is pleasantly rustic with accommodating and friendly staff. This is a great place to bring kids and even the pickiest will find something they love. There's live music on Wednesday at 9 and 10:15 pm ($6 cover), usually jazz duet and sometimes klezmer. Mezzetta is the place to go for tasty bits and bites!

Mocha-Mocha Café

489 Danforth Ave. (at Logan)
Subway: Chester
Phone: 416.778.7896
Hours: Mon-Thur & Sun 8am-10pm; until 11pm Fri & Sat
Credit cards: V, MC, Amex, Interac; Alcohol: beer & wine
Wheelchair access: yes
Average main course: $7.50

Mocha-Mocha Café provides an international selection of healthy dishes and light meals on the Danforth.

The chalkboard menu includes salads, sandwiches, crêpes and hot main courses. One of the best bets is the vegetarian club sandwich, avocado, eggplant, veggies and cheese on seven-grain bread. It's a great mix of textures and tastes, and it comes with a colourful salad and the delicious house vinaigrette. The egg salad sandwich is made fresh to order on whole wheat bread or pita. Niçoise salad is always a good choice, as is the warm brown rice salad with an Asian-inspired gingery dressing. Hot dishes include vegetarian lasagne and East African chicken stew. They serve breakfast all day every day, including fresh fruit and other crêpes, with Belgian waffles added on the weekends. The vegetable mozzarella crêpe combines eggplant, mushrooms, green onions, peppers and zucchini in a fresh tomato sauce, topped with melted cheese. They have freshly squeezed orange or carrot juice.

Owners Marijan (he is originally from the former Yugoslavia) and Mercedes Tripkovic came to Toronto from Peru where they had a pancake restaurant. In the 1990s they opened a neighbourhood restaurant on the Danforth where there were mostly Greek places. They chose an international menu oriented to wholesome and healthy food, but without compromising taste. It's a small bright and cheery place, a neighbourhood favourite with friendly staff, and a small sidewalk patio on Danforth, excellent for people watching. Food at Mocha-Mocha not only makes you feel good, it actually tastes and looks good too!

Okonomi House

23 Charles St. W. (at St. Nicholas St.)
Subway: Bloor; or 97 Yonge bus
Phone: 416.925.6176
Hours: Mon-Fri 11:30am-10pm; Sat noon-10pm;
    Sun noon-8pm
Credit cards: V, MC, Amex, Interac; Alcohol: beer
Wheelchair access: entrance yes; restroom no
Average main course: $8.50

Okonomi House is a diner-style Japanese spot in the centre of town.

The menu has a selection of Japanese comfort foods, and they are all prepared and presented beautifully, but without pretension. The miso soup is full of nori and tiny tofu cubes, warm and nourishing. The *edamame* (soy beans) are a healthful, delicious Japanese take on peanuts at the bar, and just as addictive. The *okonomi* (pancake) *yaki* (fried) is made with flour, eggs, milk, chopped cabbage, green onion, pickled ginger and a filling of your choice: beef, chicken shrimp, veggies, etc. It's topped with a BBQ sauce and mayonnaise. It's an authentic Japanese diner dish and a real deal with zing! Try the *okonomi* with sweet bay scallops and a bowl of rice for a sumptuous meal. The specials include beef, chicken, salmon, or tofu teriyaki, soba noodles with your choice of meat or seafood, and even a bento box with marinated beef and all the trimmings. All are excellent and give wonderful value. No food court chicken teriyaki can hold a candle to this version!

Okonomi House has been owned and operated by the same couple since it first opened in 1978. It won't appear in any trendy design magazines but it's clean and sparsely decorated, with a warm glow from the orange Japanese paper lanterns. There is no smoking and the music is discreet. Service is polite and demure, but efficient even during peak times. What a joy to have such unpretentious but delicious and affordable Japanese food in the heart of Toronto! It's almost too good to be true.

Olde Yorke Fish & Chips

96 Laird Drive (cor. Lea Ave.)
Subway: Donlands; then 56 Leaside bus
Phone: 416.696.9670
Hours: Mon-Sat 11am-9pm; closed Sunday
Credit cards: V, MC, Interac; Alcohol: all
Wheelchair access: yes
3305 Yonge St. (at Glenforest Rd.)
Subway: Lawrence
Phone: 416.480.1984
Classic Fish & Chips: $8.75

Olde Yorke Fish & Chips delivers classic English-style fish & chips at the original Leaside location and on Yonge north of Lawrence.

The fish (haddock, halibut, cod or Arctic whitefish) is impeccably fresh, mild and flaky, moist inside/crisp outside, and chips are fresh with skins on. The halibut is the best seller. Everything is piping hot and portions are generous. Coleslaw is excellent and malt or white vinegar and house tartar sauce are available. You can substitute salad for the chips for a slight charge if you really want to feel virtuous. There are a few other dishes available including Scottish meat pie (from White Heather Bakery in Whitby), and a hamburger. Homemade deserts are excellent if you can manage it!

Peter and Anne Feather have owned and run the original Leaside spot since1997. It is quietly and comfortably decorated. There are booths and wooden tables and chairs, as well as a bar with drinks where food is served. This is a converted historic brick house (with patio) built by the Lea for whom Leaside is named. Service is prompt and efficient and servers are well trained, pleasant, and accommodating. They are very busy and will not take reservations at peak times (5:30-8:30 Wednesday through Saturday) so expect a wait. The Yonge location is newer and larger but has exactly the same menu and management, and you may be lucky enough to avoid a wait. They do a booming take-out business including family and party packs. Fish & chips don't get any better than at Olde Yorke.

Omonia

426 Danforth Ave. (at Chester)
Subway: Chester
Phone: 416.465.2129
Hours: Sun-Thur 11am-1am; until 2am Fri & Sat
Credit cards: V, MC, Amex, Diners; Alcohol: all
Wheelchair access: yes
Average main course: $9

Omonia in the heart of the Danforth Greek area has been dishing out delicious Greek grill specialties since 1978.

Souvlakis (chicken, pork, lamb) are the overwhelming favourites. They also have a Catch of the Day special (ask about it) and a nice moussaka. For those not in a meat and potatoes mood there is a relatively new pasta menu (*makaronathes*) which offers pasta Alfredo, arabiatta, or with calamari or salmon, as well as angel hair Bolognese. The souvlaki are perfectly grilled, freshly made not stacked to sog up on a steam table for hours and hours. They're served with rice, wonderful roast potatoes, Greek salad, and all the garlic bread you can eat. Souvlaki portions are very generous, the small plates are enough for a normal person with the large version only for the Pantagruelic appetite! There are many appetizers and a selection of these make an interesting meal. If you are in a group you can just order a bundle of appetizers and mains and share family-style.

John and Toula Angelopoulos opened Omonia in 1978, one of the first Greek restaurants in the area, and Chef Apostolis Tisgaridis has been in the kitchen from the beginning. It is a large, friendly and busy place that is unpretentious and very family and kid-friendly. Staff are efficient and helpful. After a satisfying meal, you can stroll along Danforth to Logan where you will find a small public square with a statue of Alexander the Great.

Oriental Feast

3560 Victoria Park Ave. (at McNicoll Ave.), North York
Subway: Victoria Park Station
Phone: 416.498.8868
Hours: Mon-Sun 7am-2am
Credit cards: V, MC, Amex; Alcohol: all
Wheelchair access: no
1221 Markham Rd. (at Ellesmere), Scarborough
Phone: 416.289.3329
Credit cards: V, Amex; Alcohol: all
Wheelchair access: yes
Buffet: $7.95, $12.95 weekdays; $8.45, $13.95 weekends and
holidays

Oriental Feast serves a quality pan-Asian buffet with enormous choice, in North York and Scarborough.

The number of choices is almost overwhelming—soups,
typical Chinese dishes like chow mein, sweet and sour pork,
along with teppan specialties, a BBQ grill, and some Thai
specialties, among many other things. They also serve sushi
and sashimi—very popular choices. Fried Vancouver King
crabs are a seasonal specialty and are a special treat! You can
even get Peking duck—they slice it up so you can make your
own pancake rolls. The grilled fish with Thai sauce is a
delicious choice. Grilled skewers of beef or chicken are fresh,
not at all dried out, and tasty, and the veggie skewers are good
too. BBQ ribs are tender, tasty, and meaty, with a nice glaze.
It's fun to try a little of everything or go ahead and pig out on
your favourite. If you really insist, they also have chicken
wings, salad, fries, and onion rings. Fresh fruit, many different
flavours of ice cream and pie are available for a sweet ending.
Dishes are replenished frequently.

Oriental Feast manager and president Paul Chiu opened
on Victoria Park in 1997. They're affiliated with Memories of
Japan. There are fountains and a small waterfall, and it's
pleasant but not luxurious. This is a terrific place for a family,
a crowd, or if you just can't decide which kind of Asian food
you really feel like eating. Great selection! Head to Oriental
Feast for—an oriental feast of course!

Penrose Fish & Chips

600 Mount Pleasant Rd.

Bus: Eglinton Ave. E. from Eglinton subway; or Mt. Pleasant
   Rd. from St. Clair subway

Phone: 416.483.6800

Hours: Tues-Fri 11am-7pm; Sat 11am-6:30pm;
   closed Sunday and Monday

Credit cards: V, Amex, Diners; Alcohol: no

Wheelchair access: entrance yes; restroom no

Classic Fish & Chips: $6.45

Penrose Fish & Chips has been a North Toronto institution since 1950!

This is the place to go for great classic fish & chips. They serve only prime Pacific halibut and it is fresh, moist, with a light and crispy batter. They use fresh-cut PEI or Ontario potatoes. For the purist, they fry in beef drippings, which many believe make the most sinfully wonderful fish and chips. Coleslaw and bread and butter are also available if you're so inclined. They serve Seamans Old Fashioned soda pop also from PEI—try the lime rickey, orange, or birch beer. Lemon meringue pie is available only on Friday and pumpkin pie in season—both are very good.

The same family has owned and still operates Penrose's and they don't deviate from a winning formula. It is clean but décor is minimal with fluorescent lights—this is definitely not a place to linger. There are lineups at peak times, and they stop serving 15 minutes before closing time, so **be sure to get here at least a half hour before closing**. Take-out properly wrapped in newspaper is a popular option. Penrose is a smart choice for fish & chips in the true British tradition!

Pho Hung

200 Bloor St. W. (2nd Floor)
Subway: St. George
Phone: 416.563.5080
Hours: Mon-Sat 11am-10pm; closed Sunday
Credit cards: V, Interac; Alcohol: beer & wine
Wheelchair access: no
374 Spadina (at St. Andrew St.)
Subway: Spadina, then Spadina bus
Phone: 416.593.4274
Hours: 10am-10pm
Credit cards: no
Average meal-in-a-bowl soup: $5.50

Pho Hung on Bloor close to the ROM and in Chinatown is THE place to go for satisfying Vietnamese noodle soup meals, and they have great spring rolls too!

The *pho* or rice noodle soup is the star attraction and they do it beautifully here. There are 17 combinations possible mixing curried chicken, wonton, crab meat and asparagus, beef balls, etc. You might want to start with the lean beef with rice noodle the first time around and branch out. The bowl is huge and it is a completely satisfying meal—often too much for a single person. The broth is light but very tasty, the perfect foil for the noodles and other fresh ingredients. This soup can sustain life! It is warming and nourishing in winter, and yet light, easy to digest, and cooling in summer. The spring rolls are particularly well done here and very fresh. They do have other food available and it is all fine, but people really come here for the flawless pho. The hot or cold coffee with condensed milk is a sweet ending and it's worth a try.

Owners/managers Thoi and Thanh Nhuyen came to Canada in 1979, and after working in other non-food related jobs, they set up the Spadina location in 1986 and the Bloor spot in 1990. Spadina is almost in Kensington Market with a good-weather patio, while Bloor is a second floor space overlooking the Royal Ontario Museum. It's comfortable but will win no design awards, and service in both is quick, efficient and friendly. Pho Hung food just makes you feel good, and that's hard to beat!

Pho Mi Mien Tay

207 Ossington Ave. (at College)
Subway: Ossington; then bus 63 south
Phone: 416.516.1741
Hours: Sun-Thur 10am-10pm; until midnight Fri & Sat
Credit cards: no; Alcohol: beer
Wheelchair access: no
Average meal-in-a-bowl soup: $5.00

Pho Mi Mien Tay serves Vietnamese rice and egg noodle soups and great rice wrappers with fresh fillings, just west of Little Italy.

The pho (rice noodle) and mi (egg noodle) soups are meals in themselves and there are 21 different choices, all based on the same light but flavourful broth. You could start with a rare and lean beef and spread your wings in subsequent visits—they're all good and slightly different. A broad selection of vermicelli dishes is also available—vermicelli with grilled beef or shrimp etc. on the side. These are simple and good. Spring rolls are crisp with a savoury stuffing of minced pork, shrimp and vermicelli. Aside from the wonderful soups, the house specialty is any of the rice-paper wrapped dishes. The fresh ingredients arrive together with the wrapper and the accompanying lightly-pickled carrots, daikon, lettuce, and dipping sauce. Diners cook assembled ingredients on the small tabletop grill and make up the rolls to their own taste. No. 93 grilled beef combines full-flavoured beef with mint, rice paper rolls and fresh garnishes for a particularly winsome combination. Order a variety of them for a crowd and you can mix and match.

Loc Nguyen opened Pho Mi MienTay in 1999 after working in other Vietnamese restos, and this is a family-run business. Surroundings are not posh but this small place is lively and everything runs very efficiently. Customers of all ages, many of them Vietnamese, will likely be eating different selections from the menu and it is completely acceptable to discreetly point at what you may like to try. Pho Mi Mien Tay is the place for delicious and wholesome food.

Pita Break

565 Yonge St. (at Wellesley)
Subway: Wellesley
Phone: 416.968.1032
Hours: Mon-Fri 10:30am-9pm; Sat 11am-8pm; closed Sunday
   & holidays
Credit cards: V, Interac; Alcohol: no
Wheelchair access: entrance yes; restroom no
Average pita: $3.50

Pita Break is Toronto's pita/falafel champ serving the most wonderfully accessorized and delicious pita sandwiches in a neglected but historic part of Yonge Street.

The menu here is pita sandwiches in all their glory. Daily specials include a choice of two homemade soups and many sandwich combos. They make **14 kinds of pita**, baked daily without preservatives. They're all fresh and delicious, definitely superior to the usual commercial pita. You choose your pita and the ritual begins. First it is warmed briefly in the sandwich grill. The top is sliced off and you are handed the piece to munch on while you choose your main ingredient (grilled veggies, falafel or chicken) and accessories. The difference between one pita joint and another is the quality of the pita itself, and the variety of tasty treats you can add to the pita, such as coriander hot sauce, and various pickled vegetables. Pita Break goes the full distance on both counts and the results rival the best street food of Tel Aviv or the friendly competition of the falafel places on Rue des Rosiers in the Marais in Paris. You can buy the pita in packages to continue the pleasures at home.

Pita Break opened in 1995, and current owner, Mr. Hong, bought it in 1999. It's small and informal—a terrific budget-friendly place for those who want to choose all their own garnishes. Be sure to look up as you walk along Yonge. Despite decades of neglect you can see the spectacular vintage window details, brickwork and rooflines of some lovely old buildings. Pita Break has all the pieces in place for healthy and delectable food.

Poorana: Real Taste of Tradition

2692 Eglinton Ave. E. (at Brimley Rd.. S.)
Subway: Kennedy
Phone: 416.264.1600
Hours: Sun-Thur 11am-midnight; until 1am Fri & Sat
Credit cards: V, MC, Amex, Interac; Alcohol: all
Wheelchair access: yes
Average main course: $7.50

Poorana offers an extensive menu of interesting Indian specialties in Scarborough.

Samosas and pakoras are very fresh and hot, crispy outside, and served with tamarind dipping sauce. The samosas are quite spicy, the pakoras are a balanced mixture of spinach, onion, and potato in a chickpea batter. There is a nice selection of dosas and uthappam, large lacy crêpes and smaller thicker pancakes made here with rice flour and lentils, stuffed with buttery fillings, and served with chutney. Palak panner (spinach cheese curry) sliced and seared lightly, is spicy in a rich tomato sauce. The Kothu string hoppers are delicious stir-fried fine red noodles with egg, veggies or meat. It's a bit like a mild Singapore noodle. The thalis are a very good bet so you can sample more than one thing. There are some Devil's Specials that are very hot indeed! The menu is very ambitious and it also includes vindaloo, tandoor dishes, and various other specialties. Domestic, imported, and Indian beer is a perfect accompaniment.

Poorani is warm and inviting, with pleasing lighting, comfy booths and rattan tables/chairs. You can catch soccer and cricket games here on special occasions. Staff are friendly, capable and attentive. It is owned by the people who run Hoops, Epicure, and Paisano's, with primary owner and manager Raj Kandiah. Chefs Annarajah (South Indian cuisine) and Mohamrajah (formerly of Majarajah and specializing in North Indian cuisine) cover the sub-continent nicely, and there are Sri Lankan influences too. Poorama provides fine Indian food on a budget and in a dining-room environment.

Promise Restaurant

2202 Danforth Ave. (at Woodbine)
Subway: Woodbine
Phone: 416.429.6519
Hours: Tue-Sat noon-midnight
Credit cards: V, Interac; Alcohol: all
Wheelchair access: no
Average main course: $9

Promise serves authentic Ethiopian specialties on Danforth at Woodbine.

Food is served Ethiopian style. Mounds of food are placed on a communal table-sized platter of *injera*, a slightly sour, spongy crêpe-like bread made with fermented tef, a millet-like grain. Diners scoop up the food and the rich sauces with rolled up pieces of the *injera*—no utensils are required. The ancient *berberé* spices shared by Ethiopia's many ethnic groups add complex layers to the artful combinations of the ingredients. *Kitfo* is the most popular dish, lean minced beef in a spicy, rich, buttery sauce. Special *kitfo* is available only on weekends with spiced cottage cheese and collard greens on the side. There are lamb and beef stews, and a vegetarian combination, all with their own rich gravies, perfect for scooping up with the delicate *injera*. Food is spicy and very tasty, and portions are generous. A large part of the meal's pleasure is eating pieces of the sauce -infused injera covering the table, at the end of the meal—if you can manage it! Ethiopian coffee makes an ideal finish.

Owners Kidus and Jerusalem opened Promise in spring 2001 and it's very much a family operation. They are friendly, very willing to share their traditions and culture, and helpful about making selections and the logistics of how to eat the food. Décor is an interesting variety of Ethiopian crafts and it's all very comfortable. Promise provides an easy and pleasant introduction to an unfamiliar but exquisite cuisine.

Queen Mother Café

208 Queen St. W. (at McCaul St.)
Subway: Osgoode, or Queen streetcar
Phone: 416.598.4719
Hours: Mon-Sat 11:30am-1am; Sun noon-midnight
Credit cards: V, MC, Amex; Alcohol: all
Wheelchair access: entrance yes, restroom no
Average main course: $11

Queen Mother Café is a venerable haunt on the Queen Street strip, offering great atmosphere and delightful Thai and Laotian specialties.

Pad Thai (mild, medium or spicy) is done so beautifully here it's sometimes hard to order anything else! The kitchen produces a pleasing and harmonious blend of textures and tastes without the telltale ketchup of less skilled cooks. Spread your wings with the less ubiquitous but earthy and delicious traditional Northern Laos *khao soy gai*: chicken in a rich sauce of ginger, curry, coconut milk with a marinated bok choy and coriander garnish. *Ping gai* is a huge portion of crisp and toothsome marinated chicken. Appetizers can be combined to make a meal as well. The goldern triangles are crisp samosa-like pastries packed with chicken, corn, herbs and spices, with a lovely lemon/curry/yogurt dipping sauce and just the right degree of heat. Asian shrimp cakes are wonderfully firm and spicy with a sweet & sour Thai dipping sauce. Tantalizing desserts are from Dufflet Pastries and Phipps Desserts.

Queen Mother has been in business since 1978, with the same owners as the nearby Rivoli. One of the early chefs was pioneer Vanipha Southalack (she now has her own successful restos) and she introduced authentic flavours of Laos and Thailand to Toronto. Current chef Noy Phongnanouvong carries on the tradition. There's a friendly pub ambiance and even pictures of the late Queen Mother herself. A secluded back patio with a yellow awning is open Sundays. The evening menu has quite a few items which are over the *Cheap Thrills* limit but you get very good value. This is the quintessential Queen Street bistro—wonderful food and great atmosphere.

Rashnaa

307 Wellesley St. E. (near Parliament)
Subway: Wellesley or Castlefrank
Phone: 416.929.2099
Hours: Sun-Thur 11:30am-11:30pm;
    Fri & Sat 11:30am-midnight
Credit cards: V, MC, Amex, Interac; Alcohol: all
Wheelchair access: entrance yes; restroom no
Average main course: $8.95

This charming place on the northern edge of Cabbagetown serves authentic Tamil dishes from South India and Sri Lanka and other specialties.

You can make up your meal with a combination of side dishes or a main course. Spiciness can be adjusted to taste and they can usually accommodate special food needs. No preservatives or additives are used. The menu is varied but the vegetarian dishes are exceptionally good, especially the vegetarian *thali* which has rice, *roti* bread (not West Indian style) and three dishes, usually eggplant curry with a superb thick rich sauce, mild dal, and a variable third, sometimes okra. *Thali* comes with *achar*, a house carrot and onion pickle. Their butter chicken (not a Tamil specialty) is mild and deliciously saucy, and the fiery beef or chicken devil is a treat if you like things HOT. The dosas are wonderful and very popular. They have interesting lassis and *faludas* and don't miss the cardamom-scented flan-like *vatalappam* that is served cold, or the mango pudding with raisins and cashews. Spiced tea with green cardamom and milk is a perfect end to the meal.

Rashnaa (the name is related to the Sanskrit word for taste) is situated in a small house that has been converted to a cozy, comfortable and pleasant place to linger over a meal. Service is at full-size tables with glass-covered tablecloths. An enclosed courtyard in the rear is suitable for private outdoor dining in good weather. Staff are accommodating and knowledgeable. Rashnaa is a favourite of the neighbourhood and of the Tamil community because of the authentic dishes and the fine family fare.

The Real Jerk

709 Queen St. E. (at Broadview)
Subway: Broadview, then Queen streetcar;
   or Queen streetcar east
Phone: 416.463.6055
Hours: 11:30am-1am (kitchen closes at 10pm)
Credit cards: V, MC, Amex, Interac; Alcohol: all
Wheelchair access: no
Average main course: $10

The Real Jerk in Riverdale is one of Toronto's early Jamaican restaurants.

Jerk ribs and oxtail stew are among the best in town. The ribs are meltingly tender with a sweet and hot sauce. The oxtails are tender in a rich and beefy gravy. Portions are generous. Jerk chicken and jerk pork are also good (the pork gravy is stellar). The ackee and cod are tasty and well prepared, better choices than the pricier seafood. Most dishes are served with standard rice and peas and coleslaw. There is also a selection of roti and other standards as well. The delicious tropical homemade juices and deserts such as sweet potato pudding, cream pies, and tropical ice creams, are all delicious.

Real Jerk has quite an underground reputation and they play continuous reggae. The bar is a friendly neighbourhood attraction. They started as a very small café that became very popular in the 80s, but it expanded too far too fast and went through a bankruptcy in the early 90s. They now have this one location in Riverdale where they have maintained the excellent Jamaican cuisine. It's a funky and colourful place, a concrete block former bank building which they have tarted up with color, faux West Indian décor touches and beautiful Jamaican art (especially the sheet metal paintings and gorgeous menus), creating one of the most inventive and festive interiors on the Toronto restaurant scene. Go for the décor, the music, the art, but most of all go for the great food!

Rebel House

1068 Yonge St. (at Roxborough)
Subway: Rosedale
Phone: 416-927-0704
Hours: Mon-Sat 11:30am-11pm; until 10pm on Sun
Credit cards: V, MC, Amex; Alcohol: all
Wheelchair access: entrance yes; restroom no
Average main course: $10, hamburger $8.95

Rebel House is a Rosedale bar with some very fine pub-style food.

Everything is made from scratch and it shows. Cheese pennies (cheese biscuits) are an addictive house specialty. The superb beef/buffalo burger is thick, juicy, and tasty, served with superb house ancho ketchup on a real bun. You can split your side order half fries and half salad. Fries are thin-cut fresh potatoes fried in small batches of vegetable oil and they are GOOD! Mesclun salad is dressed with house vinaigrette of olive oil and raspberry wheat vinegar. They have great comfort foods like mac and cheese, and grilled cheese and bacon sandwiches. Meat loaf is a favourite—just like your mom made! The wild game sausages are more adventurous. Ask about daily specials. House-made desserts are huge and delicious, very easily shared. There's an extensive selection of imported and microbrewery beer on tap and a full bar.

Rebel House has been open since 1993 and owners Dave Logan and Bruce Roberts, and manager Diana Windsor are always close to the action, paying attention to details. Chef Kevin Beall has been in the kitchen since the beginning. The atmosphere is traditional Ontario tavern, but with appetizing food. It's an old-time bar with a young clientele, relaxed and comfortable but not glamorous. There's smoke since it's a bar and kids are allowed only on the back patio. It's hard to beat home-style food, affordable prices, and a pleasant ambiance close to the centre of town and easy public transportation. You could become a regular!

Note: A more upscale sister restaurant, Rebel Chop House, has recently opened at Bloor and Runnymede (414.927.0704).

Richmond King Noodles & Seafood Restaurant

280 West Beaver Creek (Unit 25, Highway #7), Richmond Hill
Phone: 905.882.4848
Hours: Sun-Thur 11am-1am, until 2am Fri & Sat
Credit cards: cash only; Alcohol: all
Wheelchair access: yes
Average main course: $7.50

Richmond King Noodles & Seafood Restaurant serves Chinese home-style cooking (including homemade egg noodles) from a strip mall in Richmond Hill.

This is not fancy banquet food, just simple dishes, done well. Two to three times a week they make their own noodles—long, thin, chow mein egg noodles, and won ton wrappers too. There's nothing like the taste of homemade noodles! The won ton noodle soup (*shui gow*) has four large and succulent shrimp won ton, Chinese broccoli, and, of course, those fabulous noodles, in a perfect broth—an amazing light meal in itself. Fried Singapore noodles are lightly curried, with a bit of a kick, and nicely flavoured with pork and shrimp. There are nearly 240 items on the menu, and blackboard specials too! There are many fresh, crisp veggie dishes. At the other end of the spectrum they have a pig fest for a mere $12! Or go for a mix like the *Ma po tofu*, a tasty combo of steamed tofu with pork. Order what tickles your fancy and know that it will be well prepared from fresh ingredients.

Richmond King Noodles & Seafood started out in 1974 as King Chai downtown on Dundas. Current owners Henry and Sue Lai moved to Richmond Hill and kept the Chinese name but changed the English. It's a simple place with wooden tables and no faux elegance. Everything is casual and unpretentious.

They can accommodate about 60 people and parking in the mall is a snap. True Blue noodle fans won't be disappointed at Richmond King Noodles.

Sababa Fine Foods

390 Steeles Ave. W. (bet. Yonge & Bathurst)
Subway: Steeles
Phone: 905.764.6440
Hours: Mon-Sun 11am-11pm
Credit cards: V, MC, Amex, Interac; Alcohol: all
Wheelchair access: yes
Average dinner special: $10.95

Sababa Fine Foods is a Middle Eastern restaurant, grocery and pita bakery in Thornhill.

The super-fresh pita from the adjacent bakery is, of course, front and centre at Sababa. There are a dizzying number of excellent appetizers available—a selection would make a wonderful meal and take you on a tour of many parts of the Middle East. Hummous, the exquisite Egyptian *foule mudammas*, spinach pie, stuffed vine leaves and more—they've got the works! The falafel and shawarma are extremely popular and they're fresh and delicious! Dinners include a main course, rice or fries, salad, and a choice of appetizer—a terrific deal. The shish kebab is tender, moist lamb or beef that is perfectly grilled. The lamb chops and chicken or shrimp kebabs are also grilled beautifully, and the veal liver steak is a tender treat. Portions are very generous but you can order light dinner combos if you wish. Baklava is the perfect ending.

Sam Azar opened Sababa in 1987, his fourth Toronto restaurant since 1975. It grew and it's now a veritable food emporium: a large restaurant, a Middle Eastern grocery and a pita bakery. Sam's four sons run the operation but he still keeps his hand in. Sababa is spacious, spotlessly clean, well organized and well run. The restaurant has light wood panelling and tables and pleasant lighting. There are decorative brass plates on the walls and a large decorative camel and elephant add a nice touch. Service is pleasant and efficient. This is a lovely place to go for a delightful Middle Eastern dinner.

Salad King Thai Cuisine

335 Yonge St.
Subway: Dundas
Phone: 416.971.5157
Hours: Mon-Sat 11am-9:30pm; Closed Sundays & holidays
Credit cards: V, MC, Interac; Alcohol: beer
Wheelchair access: entrance yes; restroom no
Average main course: $6.50

Head to cafeteria-style Salad King Thai Cuisine on Yonge near Ryerson for wonderful Thai food with real heat!

Food here is Hot! You can order your food mild, medium, nice, and from 1 chili to 20. Even mild is quite a bit spicier than equivalents elsewhere, so beware—it's hard to eat food past 3 chilis, even for the diehard chilihead! The weekly specials are posted on the board near the door and they are incredible deals. Chicken lemongrass soup is a heart-warming spicy broth full of flavour, chicken, veggies, lime leaves, basil, and lemongrass—maybe better than your grandmother's chicken soup! Thai green curry chicken (very popular) is made with the house-made curry paste and it's awesome! Spring rolls are fresh, light, and crisp. Sesame shrimp is perfectly stir-fried with peppers, eggplant and carrots in a creamy brown sauce rich with garlic, peanuts and sesame seeds. Portions are generous, and it's hard to choose since everything is good. Work your way through the menu!

Ernest and Linda Liu opened this bustling noisy place in 1991 and it's always busy. Everyone is polite and the whole operation is efficient. Décor is non-existant—formica tables and fake plants. You order, pay at the counter, and receive a number for each dish. You have to pay attention and when your number is called you pick up the dishes at a self-service window. People go to Salad King Thai Cuisine for the exceptional Thai food that also happens to be very easy on the wallet. This is some of the best Thai food in Toronto.

Sashimi House

2038 Sheppard Ave. E. (at Brian Dr.)
Subway: Sheppard, then Sheppard east bus
Phone: 416.495.1208
Hours: Mon-Sun 11am-11pm
Credit cards: V, Interac; Alcohol: all
Wheelchair access: yes
Average main course: $9

Sashimi House is a jewel of a place for sushi and other Japanese treats on Sheppard East in North York.

The quality of the fish is impeccable. Sushi and sashimi are available by the piece or in combos, beautifully prepared by practiced hands and utterly fresh. You can choose nigiri sushi, sashimi, hand roll, or maki for salmon, surf clam, tuna, yellowtail, octopus, cuttlefish, scallop, flying fish egg, sea urchin, etc. The spicy tuna roll is a real winner, and their California rolls never fall apart. Nigiri BBQ eel is only $1.25 a piece and it's mouth-watering good. If you're not a sushi fan there are combos like the fantastic chicken teriyaki and shrimp tempura (there are six to choose from), or wholesome and soothing noodle meals. They have appetizer portions of seafood or *wakame* sunomomo, wonderful gyozo dumplings, veggie tempura and miso soup. They also do catering and party trays at really reasonable prices—be sure to call ahead.

Sashimi House has been open since 1994, expanding to a second dining room in 1998. Owner Alan Seto cooks the hot dishes and a variety of sushi chefs are on view in the newer dining room. The original space is favored by the "old timers" but it's all comfortable and friendly. Décor is simple, and everyone loves the blowfish hanging from the ceiling. It's usually busy, especially at lunch where there's often a lineup, and take-out is very popular. This is a favourite spot for sushi fanatics from Scarborough to Missisauga, and it's well worth the trip! Sashimi House may be Toronto's best value for your sushi dollar!

Sensation Café

26 Baldwin St. (at Henry St.)
Subway: Queen's Park, or College streetcar
Phone: 416.348.0731
Hours: Mon-Sun 11:30am-11pm; until midnight
  during summer
Credit cards: V, MC; Alcohol: all
Wheelchair access: no
Average main course: $9

Sensation Café in Baldwin Village has a limited but delicious Italian menu and luscious desserts.

The house-made daily soups are artful combos like curried cream of broccoli, and they are definitely worth a try. Sandwiches are meal-sized and include roasted vegetables, chicken, or ham, and cheese. They do pasta well, and the pasta specials of the day are always an excellent bet. Go for the excellent linguine with mussels if it's on offer. Golden mussels are plump, tender morsels in a creamy curry sauce—divine when it is sopped up with crusty bread! Individual thin-crust Mediterranean pizza with goat cheese with pesto is a good vegetarian option. Creamy, spicy Cajun risotto and grilled chicken breast with apple are also popular choices. Weekend brunch specials include eggs Benedict and eggs Natasha (with smoked salmon instead of ham). Desserts are from Dufflet's Bakery, with the raspberry mousse cake a particular favourite here. Coffee choices are smooth and delicious, with lattes served in huge bowls.

Jean Park opened Sensation originally as a dessert café in 1991. The dessert display is still the centrepiece of the restaurant, and they are very tempting indeed! Like the rest of Baldwin Village it can be very busy at lunch. The pleasant café ambiance is somewhere between a diner and a dining room. The patio out front gives a front-row view of Baldwin Street, with a tree and hanging flower baskets. Service is excellent and the staff are young and funky. Sensation offers great value for your dining dollar with real food at excellent prices and Baldwin Street café ambiance.

Skylark Restaurant

1433 Gerrard St. E. (at Ashdale Ave.)
Subway: Coxwell, or Carlton streetcar
Phone: 416.469.1500
Hours: Mon-Sun 12pm-10pm
Credit cards: V, MC, Amex; Alcohol: all
Wheelchair access: no
Buffet: $7.99

Skylark has an affordable North Indian buffet on the Little India strip on Gerrard East.

The Real Deal here is the buffet. There are other items on the menu but almost everyone eats from the buffet which is frequently replenished. It includes three kinds of curry (mixed vegetable, mutton, and chicken), *aloo gobi* (cauliflower and potatoes cooked in mild Indian spices), *dal makhnai* (warm, buttery lentils), and North Indian standards like butter and tandoori chicken. There's also pulao rice and waiters replenish the naan regularly so you can use it to soak up the delicious rich sauces. The butter chicken is exquisite. Plus there are fresh salads, relishes, papadams and chutneys. Desert is ice cream and *gulab jam*, deep-fried cheese balls soaked in sweet syrup. Everything tastes good, even late in the evening. Curries are mild but you can add your own heat if you wish. Cold Kingfisher Indian beer is the perfect accompaniment.

Skylark has been around since the mid 1970s and there are many regular customers. They've worked out all the details of how to do this kind of buffet very well. Skylark turns out quality food in quantity, and they have courteous and efficient staff. The décor is nondescript but not at all unpleasant. Families, couples, and single diners are all welcome and comfortable here. This is satisfying North Indian food at bargain prices.

Songha Thai Cuisine

2998 Dundas St. W. (at Keele)
Subway: Keele, then Annette bus
Phone: 416.760.8035
Hours: Tue-Sat noon-10pm; Sun 5pm-10pm; closed Monday
Credit cards: V, MC; Alcohol: all
Wheelchair access: yes
Average main course: $7.50

Songha Thai Cuisine is a popular neighbourhood restaurant serving real Thai food on Dundas West.

There are deft touches like fresh sweet basil, green onion and cilantro finishes to most dishes, and the food has the complex layering of all good Thai food. Crisp fresh vegetables are generous in virtually all the dishes. You can choose from vegetarian, chicken, beef, pork, or seafood specialties in the extensive menu. The chicken rice noodle soup is excellent, but then all the soups are good—flavourful broth chock full of chicken, beef, shrimp, seafood or tofu, noodles, and all kinds of other tasty goodies. The lemongrass soups with or without coconut are also recommended. The pad Thai is very nicely done, a blend of taste and texture, and available in vegetarian and non-vegetarian versions. They have some wonderful tamarind dishes—the *kai makam* (chicken) or *goong makam* (shrimp) are both excellent choices. The Thai-style vegetarian spring rolls are light and crisp appetizers or snacks. There are also some typically Thai salads. Lunch specials are a real deal with full meals for $5.95.

Cuc and Toan Lee opened Songha Thai Cuisine in 1994. Cuc cooks the food of her native Thailand and Toan, an engineer and artist, is responsible for the pleasant décor. This family business became so popular that they doubled in size a few years ago. Service is friendly and very fast—you might want to order things in stages. They have a loyal clientele who keep coming back for those true Thai tastes, the warm welcome, and the excellent value.

Spadina Garden

116 Dundas St. W. (at Bay)
Subway: Dundas
Phone: 416.977.3413
Hours: Mon-Fri 11:30am-9:30pm; Sat noon-10pm; Sun 4pm-
  10pm
Credit cards: V, MC, Amex, Interac; Alcohol: all
Wheelchair access: yes
Average main course: $8.95

Spadina Garden has fabulous Chinese/Szechuan food—it's
at Dundas and Bay despite its name.

You'll find all your favourites here and they do them all
very well. There's a great selection of meal combos for
$11.95—a real deal! You can order individual dishes too.
Everything is prepared on demand—it doesn't sit for hours
on a steam table. Spiciness is clearly marked, but they're
pleased to make adjustments. The hot spicy peanut chicken
is to die for, with plenty of crunchy peanuts and bean sprouts
in a luscious spicy sauce. This is really addictive stuff! Hunan
beef is melt-in-your-mouth tender and the sauce is wonderful.
Chicken with black bean sauce and the hot garlic beef with
mixed vegetables are also good choices. Crispy ginger chicken
is another big favourite.

The Wong and Chen family opened Spadina Garden in
1983 on Spadina. They moved to Dundas in 1989, but kept
the name. Chef Winne Wong was born in India and came to
Canada in 1980. Many of her nine brothers and sisters have
other restaurants in Toronto. This is very much a family
business and everything runs smoothly. It's very nicely set
up with tablecloths and comfortable chairs. Décor is discreet
with neutral colours, large Chinese prints on the walls, and
small red paper lanterns. It's a very popular place with a loyal
clientele so it can be crowded and noisy, especially at lunch,
but service is friendly, and quick. Spadina Garden is a great
downtown choice for Chinese/Szechuan food.

sPaHa modern bistro

66 Harbord St. (at Spadina)
Subway: Spadina, or Harbord bus
Phone: 416.260.6133
Hours: Sun-Thur 10:30am-midnight; until 2am Fri & Sat
Credit cards: V, MC, Amex, Interac; Alcohol: all
Wheelchair access: yes
Average main course: $9.50 (except fish & steak)

sPaHa serves updated bistro-style food in a light-filled minimalist space at SPAdina and HArbord near the University of Toronto.

The menu includes breakfast, bistro-style choices, and higher-end dishes that are beyond the *Cheap Thrills* guidelines, but there are plenty of budget choices. Soups are nicely crafted and generous—to make a meal combine with an appetizer like the wonderful citrus chicken wings. Niçoise salad with fine dressing is a good choice for lunch, and it's also available with beautifully poached salmon. Sandwiches are on crusty/chewy sourdough bread—add fries or salad for $2. The roast beef sandwich (lean and rare) with caramelized onions is yummy. Steamed mussels are really good. Burgers are big and juicy, and fresh-cut shoestring fries are perfect. Main courses include penne with wild mushroom cream sauce and chicken, and in winter cassoulet and duck confit. Desserts are decadent and can be shared. Smooth Italian espresso comes from a gorgeous Gaggia machine.

Anwar Mukhayesh (see Kensington Kitchen) designed and opened sPaHa in 2000 on this ground floor of the U of T graduate student residence. It gets rave reviews for postmodern minimalist design, and it is indeed no diner! But the design hoopla belies the menu, and the unpretentious clientele who like the light and clean organic feel of the place and the reasonable prices for good food. They're set up for high-speed wireless—it's free for now but will eventually be $4-$5/hour. sPaHa is a great place to eat well or to linger over an espresso—and you can do it even if you're on a budget.

Swatow Restaurant

309 Spadina Ave. (at Darcy St.)
Subway: Spadina, then Spadina bus; or College streetcar
Phone: 416.977.0601
Hours: Sun-Thur 11:30am-2am; until 4:30am Fri & Sat
Credit cards: cash only; Alcohol: no
Wheelchair access: no
Average main course: $8

Swatow in Chinatown is home to some of the best Chinese food in Toronto.

The menu is varied, with many distinctive taste twists. They make everything from scratch and are very accommodating about amending any dish to your taste and degree of heat. Soups are made in full view, and if you're there at the right moment you can watch them make the delicious dumplings that are served panfried. Shrimp dumpling soup pairs lovely dumplings with a light flavourful broth, an addictive Asian version of Mom's chicken soup! The house specialty, Swatow duck, is boneless, deep-fried and served sliced, with a special sauce with nuanced layers of taste and texture. The sizzling platters (beef tenderloin, chicken with satay, seafood and more) are recommended. Any of the black bean sauce dishes are a good bet, especially the beef. Check out other tables, and don't hesitate to ask for what appeals to you. Be adventurous, and you just may be glad you did!

Peter Li opened Swatow in 1979, and his partner of 10 years, Jerry Au, is the talented chef. It's a popular destination for authentic Chinese cooking aficionados from all over Toronto. Swatow (Chaochow or Chiuchow) is a coastal city in Canton (Kwangtung). It has its own distinctive cooking style but the menu here is more of an eclectic mix, including a touch of hot spice. Service is fast and staff are helpful. This small, brightly-lit space is noisy, and often crowded. It looks a bit like a dive, but make no mistake, Swatow is about fabulous food. Once you've eaten here you are sure to be back.

Tacos el Asador

690 Bloor St. W. (at Clinton)
Subway: Christie
Phone: 416.538.9747
Hours: Mon-Tue & Thur-Sat noon-9pm; Sun 2pm-6pm;
    closed Wednesday
Credit cards: cash only; Alcohol: beer
Wheelchair access: no
Average combo: $6.50

This is the right place for a taste of Salvadoran street food, just north of Little Italy.

The cuisine is simple and satisfying. You put together a meal by combining the appropriate number of small snacks. The whole thing is pulled together by the pink pickled veggies that you eat with everything. Burritos are the largest of the snacks with a soft flour tortilla holding the tasty beef, chicken, pork, or vegetarian filling—these are smaller than the Mexican burritos we see more often. Soft or crispy tacos are filled with lettuce, tomato, fresh cheese and chorizo, beef or chicken. You will want to eat more than one of the small quesadillas oozing delicious melted cheese. Onion and cilantro adds a pleasing texture to the chunky guacamole. The special Salvadoran touch is the pupusas (cheese/bean, squash or pork)—a stuffed cornflour pancake that comes alive with the pickle and salsa. The salsas liven up everything and they're available mild, medium, and completely incendiary (beware!).

Salvador Gonzales opened Tacos el Asador in 1992. The cooking is done by his wife Elena and her sister Lady. This is a small, lively and friendly place but amenities are limited, and it is more a place to pick up your food and move on rather than a place to linger. At Tacos el Asador you can eat for very little money while introducing yourself to some of the basics of Salvadoran street food.

Tavola Calda

671 College St. (at Beatrice)
Subway: College, then College streetcar
Phone: 416.536.8328
Hours: Tue-Sun 11am-11pm (closed Sunday in winter)
Credit cards: V, MC, Amex, Interac; Alcohol: all
Wheelchair access: yes
Average main course: $7, panini $6

Tavola Calda serves home-style Italian food on the College Street strip.

The menu includes only down-to-earth Italian home-style cooking. They have eight panini choices and you can pay a little more for extra toppings like grilled eggplant, roasted red peppers, artichokes, and provolone. The breaded veal cutlet panini is a popular and wonderful choice for a lovely lunch or a light dinner. The main courses and salads come in regular and (truly) large. It's all wonderful and so hard to choose! Cheese ravioli are house-made, al dente pillows of pasta with fluffy ricotta filling. They are mind-blowingly good with pan-fried rapini on the side. Spezzatino, earthy veal stew served over rice, is divine! Then there's veal cutlet, flawless eggplant parmesan, roast chicken, spaghetti with meatballs, not to mention a small selection of interesting salads. They serve Italian sodas and fruit nectars, and good espresso. The biscotti are delicious and there are more substantial desserts if you can manage it, but you may just want to walk a bit and have some fruit later on. They also have an Italian-style brunch on weekends until 4.

Tavola Calda was opened in 1996 by Mary Lanzillotto and her son Pat. She cooks and he takes care of the front. They expanded the really tiny original space in 2000 and it is now larger and much more pleasant and comfortable. In good weather the patio is usually crowded. This is the utterly unpretentious, but lovingly prepared and wonderful, REAL food of a Southern Italian home kitchen—and it just makes you feel good.

Timothy's Tikka House

556 Parliament St. (at Wellesley St.)
Bus: Parliament St. bus, or Carlton streetcar
Phone: 416.964.7583
Hours: Mon-Fri 11am-3pm & 5pm-11pm; Sat noon-11pm;
   Sun 4pm-10pm
Credit cards: V, MC, Amex, Interac; Alcohol: all
Wheelchair access: yes
Average main course: $8.95

Timothy's Tikka House in Cabbagetown serves traditional
North Indian specialties.

   The level of heat is quite high, so the faint-hearted should
indicate clearly that you want mild spicing. They have three
kinds of BBQ chicken: traditional charbroiled North-
American, tandoori style with long marination in a special
yogurt mixture, and "Timmy Cued" with an Indian-inspired
marinade including tomato and ginger, that is also
charbroiled. They're all delicious and different from each
other. Timothy's special BBQ sauce (mild, medium, or hot)
is curry-based with onions, garlic, ginger, tomatoes and secret
spices, and it is special. Vegetarian dishes are excellent,
especially *bengan bhartha*, eggplant roasted in clay then
cooked with peas and tomatoes, and house-made *saag paneer*.
Butter chicken is a favourite—boneless tandoori cooked in
cream, onions, and tomato with a dash of mint. They offer a
full range of curries, nicely spiced with rich, flavourful sauces.
Chicken tikka roll or minced lamb roll (both in a roti wrap)
are both delicious. Rose-scented and mango lassis are
spectacular. Lamb vindaloo is a luscious fiery delight from
Goa on the west coast of India. Portions are generous but
you will want to order nan bread or rice to round things out.

   Timothy's opened in 1981 and current owners Ravinder
Kapoor and master chef Balraj Awathi have been here since
1997. This neighbourhood favourite has recently been
renovated and it's fresh and casual. Service is excellent. If
you're looking for home style North Indian cooking done
with polish and flair, this is the place for you!

Udupi Palace

1460 Gerrard St. E. (bet. Rhodes & Craven)
Subway: Coxwell, or Carlton streetcar
Phone: 416.405.8189
Hours: Sun-Thur noon-10pm; until 11pm Fri & Sat
Credit cards: V, MC, Amex, Interac; Alcohol: no
Wheelchair access: entrance yes; restroom no
Average combo dinner: $9

Udupi Palace is a vegetarian restaurant with wholesome South Indian specialties in Little India.

The menu centres around dosas, uthapam, and curries. Dosas and uthapam are both made with a batter of fermented rice paste and lentils. Dosas are very large (up to 24 inches!) thin lacy crêpes. The crêpe is used as a wrap/scoop for a variety of fillings. Uthapam are thicker and more like pancakes. Accompanying dips and chutneys are very complementary and pull the whole thing together. They're all good and it's fun to go in a group and order a few. Unless you've become a dosa addict, other good options are the curries or the thali combo. There are a few items with dairy but most of the menu is vegan.

Owner Hubert d'Mello is from Bombay, and he opened the first Udupi Palace in the U.S. in 1996. This first Canadian venture with chef Narian Moorthi opened in October 2001, one of a small number of similar places started by three friends. Udupi is a city in Mangalore, South India where dosas originated. It's non-smoking, very spacious, and uncluttered. Staff are attentive and helpful explaining how it all works. It's a good space to linger and to talk, and there's plenty of room for kids to spread out. It's a great ending to a day wandering around nearby Indian specialty stores. Udupi Palace provides a wonderful introduction to wholesome and delicious vegetarian versions of South Indian specialties, dosas and uthapam.

United Bakers Dairy Restaurant

506 Lawrence Ave. W. (Lawrence Plaza)
Subway: Lawrence
Phone: 416.789.0519
Hours: Mon-Sun 7am-9pm
Credit cards: V, MC; Alcohol: no
Wheelchair access: no
Average main course: $8.50

United Bakers is an old Toronto dairy deli (New York-style) in the Lawrence Plaza.

United Bakers' menu is home-style European-Jewish food. Breakfast includes eggs (plain, with lox, cheese, and as different kinds of omelettes), waffles, pancakes, French toast, and, of course, bagels with cream cheese and lox. For lunch or dinner there are soups, salads, fish and vegetarian dinners and specialties like latkes, gefilte fish, blintzes and cabbage rolls. Everything is fresh, filling, and tasty, nothing is very spicy, or unusual. Soups are hearty and satisfying—barley/bean is served on Tuesday and Saturday, cold or hot beet borscht every day, and potato on Wednesday and Sunday. The macaroni and cheese is cheesy and comforting. Scoops of chopped egg, coleslaw, potato salad, tuna and egg salad sit ever so primly on platters, and are served with a bagel or bread. Tuna melts are irresistible. The scent of baked carp wafts over the table with easy familiarity. Desserts are a delicious baked apple, rice pudding, or bananas with sour cream or yogurt. They have a kid's menu and serve old-fashioned milkshakes.

The Ladovsky family opened the original restaurant in 1912 on Spadina, in the Jewish immigrant community. The original is gone, but this version is owned by the third generation. It has a warm and familiar ambiance. It can get loud but it's not boisterous. It's smoke-free. You sometimes see four generations sharing busy Sunday lunch (there are lineups) or 6 pm dinners in comfortable booths. United Bakers Dairy Restaurant has been keeping customers happy with this food for generations, and it still has appeal across all generations.

Urban Thai

638 College St. (at Grace St.)
Streetcar: College
Phone: 416.535.8424
Hours: Mon-Wed 4pm-10:30pm; Thur-Sat noon-midnight;
  Sun 4pm-10pm
Credit cards: V, MC, Amex, Interac; Alcohol: all
Wheelchair access: no
1959 Queen St. E. (at Woodbine)
Subway: Woodbine, or Queen streetcar east
Phone: 416.691.2999
Hours: Mon-Sun 11:30am-11:30pm
Wheelchair access: entrance yes; restroom no
Average main course: $9.95

Urban Thai offers Thai dining on a budget in Little Italy and in the Beaches.

The soups and salads are great. Lemon grass shrimp soup is a huge spicy bowl with a complex range of perfectly blended and complementary flavours offsetting the chili heat—mmmm! Pass on the unexceptional appetizers because there are too many other great things to eat here. Green mango salad or glass noodle seafood salad are always a treat, and especially so in warm weather. The green curry chicken is as good as you get in Toronto, superbly sweet and spicy with loads of chicken in a rich flavour-packed sauce that's especially good with coconut rice. You won't go wrong with pad Thai in any of its incarnations (chicken & shrimp, vegetarian, chicken, etc.). Savoury cashew chicken is a large serving including cashews, of course, and crisp vegetables in a sensational sweet garlic orange sauce finished with fresh coriander. Portions are generous and pork is not served.

Chan Senatherajah, who opened Urban Thai in 2001, is Sri Lankan and he also owns Friendly Thai. It's a popular quality Thai place with a dining room atmosphere and budget prices. It's quiet with candles and soft lighting, but funky and modern. Service is fast and unobtrusive by competent and knowledgeable staff. This food is superb, some of the most flavourful Thai cooking in Toronto, and that's quite a feat at these unpretentious prices.

Wally's Restaurant

5088 Dundas St. W. (at Kipling St.)
Subway: Kipling
Phone: 416.234.9792
Hours: Tue-Sun 11am-9pm; closed Monday
Credit cards: V, MC, Amex, Interac; Alcohol: all
Wheelchair access: yes
Average main course: $8.50

Wally's is an old-time Eastern European place on Dundas West at Kipling.

Meals come with dense European rye bread and butter and a generous portion of steamed vegetables. Borscht is rich and thick with beets, shredded cabbage, carrots, and fresh dill in a real beef broth. The house specialties are Wiener schnitzel, pierogies, and cabbage rolls. Pierogies are large, tender dumplings pan-fried in butter, with melt-in-your-mouth potato and cheese filling. The schnitzel is thin and tender with a light, crisp breading. Cabbage rolls are all your heart desires! The cabbage wrapping still has a slight crunch, the rice and beef (chopped not ground beef) filling is tasty and simply flavoured, and the tomato sauce has a slight vinegar tang. Potato salad is the perfect choice for a side dish, a mixture of chunky potatoes, shredded carrot, pepper, and green onions in light vinegar dressing. The house platter for two is a real pig-out selection of everything. German beer on tap goes well with everything. The warm Viennese strudel (cakey with big chunks of apple) is a fitting dessert if you can manage it. Lunch specials are a bargain for the value.

Wally's has been around for over 35 years! Mia Stan has been the owner since 1998, and her son Michael is the manager. The chef is Charlie, the previous owner, and he is in the kitchen every day. Wally's is clean, warm, and inviting and there is no smoking. It can be busy at peak times, especially Friday and Saturday. This family business is well organized and well run. Kids are definitely welcome. Wally's is for good food and lots of it, at low prices.

Yueh Tung

126 Elizabeth St. (at Dundas St. W.)
Subway: Dundas
Phone: 416.977.0933
Hours: Mon-Thur 11:30am-11:30pm; until 1am Fri;
    Sat noon-1am; Sun noon-11pm
Credit cards: V, Interac; Alcohol: all
Wheelchair access: yes
Average main course: $7.95

Yueh Tung near the Eaton Centre is a long-time favourite, with a full Chinese menu.

The menu lists 254 dishes, including egg rolls, soups, BBQ meats, sweet and sour, meat dishes with veggies, tofu combos, seafood, sizzling dishes, noodles, and chow mein. They have all the standards, including many hot and spicy dishes. Portions are large and food is freshly prepared to order by an experienced and expert kitchen. Very affordable hot and sour soup is a delightful medley of taste and texture. House specialties include chow mein, spicy chili chicken, and spicy, sizzling, ginger-laced Manchurian chicken. Veggies are crisp and sauces are well composed and generous. Seasonal lobster and crab specialties are a special treat and are very popular. Curry-laced Singapore noodles are also a good choice. A wide selection of interesting combination dinners offers great food and great value. Lunch is mobbed and is an outstanding value ($4.95-$5.50) with quick and efficient service. Refreshing orange slices finish things off very well.

Yueh Tung has been in this area (3 locations within a block) since 1979, and in its present large and simply decorated space since 1999. Michael Liu took over in 1987. He's very hands-on and he keeps old menu favourites but makes innovations too. They have about 100 seats and can get very busy, but it's all well organized and staff are efficient and friendly. Reservations are for evenings only, and it's recommended. Yueh Tung is an old Toronto favourite for Chinese food, and they keep a loyal clientele by providing a diverse selection of quality food at great prices.

Specialty Index

Family
Diana Sweets 37
Jawny Bakers 56

Fish & Chips
Olde Yorke Fish & Chips 76
Penrose Fish & Chips 79

Greek
Greek Odyssey Souvlaki 48
Omonia 77

Guyanese
Coconut Grove Roti Shop 31

Hungarian
Country Style 32

Indian
Annapurna 18
Biryani House 23
Jodhpore Club 58
Poorana: Real Taste of Tradition 83
Rashnaa 86
Skylark 94
Timothy's Tikka House 101
Udupi Palace 102

Iranian
Darvish 36

Italian
Amato 17
Bitondo 22
Ferro 43
Grano 47
John's Classic Pizza 59
Magic Oven 70
Mamma's Pizza 71
Tavola Calda 100

Japanese
Daily Sushi 34
Ho Su Bistro 53
Izmi Sushi 55
Kon-nichi-wa Deli 65
Okonomi House 75
Sashimi House 92

Jamaican
Real Jerk 87

Jewish
United Bakers Dairy 103

Korean
Ho Su Bistro 53

Laotian
Queen Mother Café 85

Malaysian
Jean's Fine Foods Catering 57

Mauritian
Blue Bay Café 24

Mexican
El Paisano Taqueria 39
El Sol 40

Middle Eastern
Kensington Kitchen 63
Mezzetta Café 73
Pita Break 82
Sababa Fine Foods 90

Pakistani
Lahore Tikka House 66

Peruvian
Caramba Restaurant 27

Portuguese
Churrasco Villa 30

Pub
Artful Dodger 19
Bishop & the Belcher 21
Feathers Brewpub 42
Hair of the Dog 51
Rebel House 88

Salvadoran
Tacos el Asador 99

Sri Lanka
Rashnaa 86

Tamil
Rashnaa 86

Thai
Green Mango 49
Jean's Fine Foods
  Catering 57
Queen Mother Cafe 111
Salad King Thai
  Cuisine 91
Songha Thai Cuisine 95
Urban Thai 104

Trinidadian
Island Foods 54

Vegetarian
Annapurna 18
Gourmet Vegetarian 46
Juice for Life 60

Vietnamese
Dai Nam 33
Pho Hung 80
Pho Mi Mien Tay 81

West Indian
Island Foods 54
Real Jerk 87

Neighbourhood Index

Restaurant Web Sites

Café Diplomatico
www.menupalace.com/diplomatico

Centre Street Deli
www.menupalace.com/centrestreetdeli

Ethiopian House
www.ethiopianhouse.com

Feathers Brewpub
http://home.istar.ca/~feathers/feathers.shtml

Bella! Did You Eat? - Free Times Café
www.thefreetimescafe.netfirms.com/menu.html

Grano
www.grano.ca

Green Mango
www.greenmango.ca

Juice for Life
www.juiceforlife.com

Lick's Homeburgers & Ice Cream
www.lickshomeburgers.com

Magic Oven
www.magicoven.com

Mamma's Pizza
www.mammaspizza.com

The Real Jerk
www.therealjerk.com

Sababa Fine Foods
www.sababafoods.com

Salad King Thai Cuisine
www.saladking.com

Send us Your Suggestions

Send us your suggestions for the next edition of
Cheap Thrills Toronto.

Visit us on the Web:

www.vehiculepress.com

www.cheapthrillsguides.com

Véhicule Press